Christian Heroes: Then & Now

ROWLAND BINGHAM

Into Africa's Interior

Christian Heroes: Then & Now

ROWLAND BINGHAM

Into Africa's Interior

JANET & GEOFF BENGE

YWAM Publishing is the publishing ministry of Youth With A Mission (YWAM), an international missionary organization of Christians from many denominations dedicated to presenting Jesus Christ to this generation. To this end, YWAM has focused its efforts in three main areas: (1) training and equipping believers for their part in fulfilling the Great Commission (Matthew 28:19), (2) personal evangelism, and (3) mercy ministry (medical and relief work).

For a free catalog of books and materials, call (425) 771-1153 or (800) 922-2143. Visit us online at www.ywampublishing.com.

Rowland Bingham: Into Africa's Interior

Published by YWAM Publishing
a ministry of Youth With A Mission
P.O. Box 55787, Seattle, WA 98155-0787

Library of Congress Cataloging-in-Publication Data
Benge, Janet, 1958–
Rowland Bingham : into Africa's interior / by Janet and Geoff Benge.
p. cm. — (Christian heroes, then & now)
Includes bibliographical references.
ISBN 1-57658-282-5
1. Bingham, Rowland V., 1872–1942—Juvenile literature.
2. Missionaries—Sudan (Region)—Biography—Juvenile literature.
3. Sudan Interior Mission—Biography—Juvenile literature.
4. Missionaries—Canada—Biography—Juvenile literature. I. Benge, Geoff, 1954– II. Title. III. Series.
BV3625.S812B46 2003
266'.0092—dc21 2002154360

Sixth printing 2022

ISBN 978-1-57658-282-4 (paperback)
ISBN 978-1-57658-618-1 (e-book)

Printed in the United States of America

Christian Heroes: Then & Now

Adoniram Judson
Albert Schweitzer
Amy Carmichael
Betty Greene
Brother Andrew
Cameron Townsend
Charles Mulli
Clarence Jones
Corrie ten Boom
Count Zinzendorf
C. S. Lewis
C. T. Studd
David Bussau
David Livingstone
Dietrich Bonhoeffer
D. L. Moody
Elisabeth Elliot
Eric Liddell
Florence Young
Francis Asbury
George Müller
Gladys Aylward
Helen Roseveare
Hudson Taylor
Ida Scudder
Isobel Kuhn
Jacob DeShazer
Jim Elliot
John Flynn
John Newton
John Wesley
John Williams
Jonathan Goforth
Klaus-Dieter John
Lillian Trasher
Loren Cunningham
Lottie Moon
Mary Slessor
Mildred Cable
Nate Saint
Norman Grubb
Paul Brand
Rachel Saint
Richard Wurmbrand
Rowland Bingham
Samuel Zwemer
Sundar Singh
Wilfred Grenfell
William Booth
William Carey

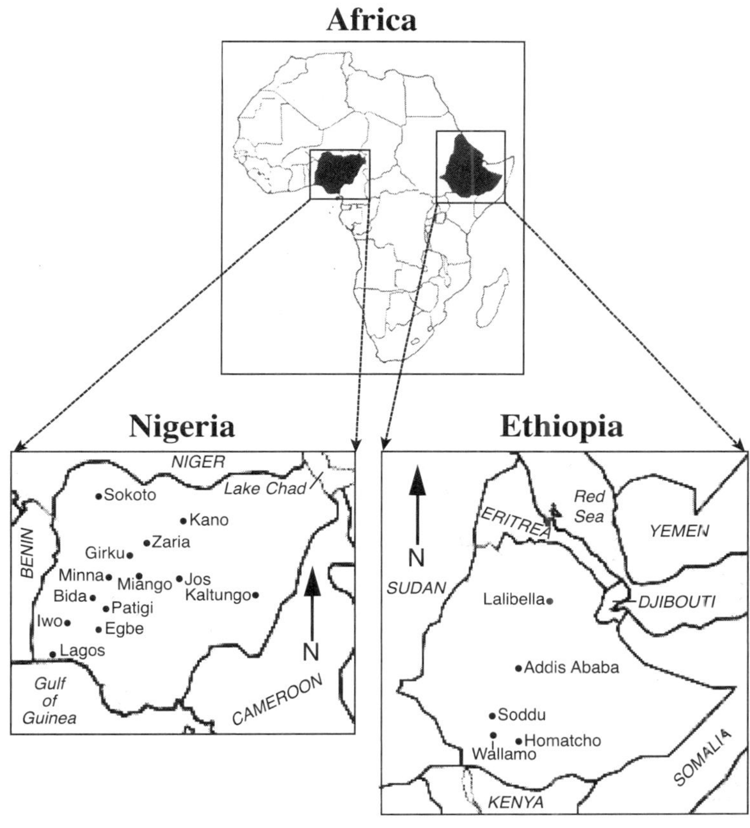
Africa
Nigeria
NIGER
Lake Chad
Sokoto
Kano
Zaria
Girku
BENIN
Minna
Miango
Jos
Kaltungo
Bida
Patigi
Iwo
Egbe
Lagos
N
Gulf of Guinea
CAMEROON
Ethiopia
N
Red Sea
ERITREA
YEMEN
SUDAN
Lalibella
DJIBOUTI
Addis Ababa
Soddu
Homatcho
Wallamo
SOMALIA
KENYA

Contents

Chapter 1

Some Kind of Magic

Rowland Bingham watched two burly, richly dressed Africans stroll into the courtyard. Long, curved silver swords dangled from the men's belts and glinted in the sunlight. At the sight of Rowland, the men drew their swords and strode toward the bench where he and his interpreter sat waiting to see the king.

The men uttered a storm of words Rowland couldn't understand, but he understood their threatening voices and sharp swords well enough. The African he had hired to be his translator shouted back, and the two strangers lifted their swords and waved them in the air.

Rowland felt strangely calm, given the situation. He knew he was a lone white man, an unwelcome missionary in the palace of the Muslim king of Iwo. The nearest help was a four-day walk away, much too far to be of any practical use to him. He was at the mercy of the king's command.

Just when Rowland thought the men were going to attack, a courtier arrived. He announced that the king would now see Rowland and motioned for Rowland to follow him.

"Be strong and of good courage," Rowland whispered to his interpreter, also a believer, as they walked through the lavishly decorated halls of the palace. "Be not afraid, but speak and hold not thy peace, for I am with thee, and no man shall set on thee to hurt thee." This was a verse from his Bible reading that morning, one he believed was a promise that would keep them safe.

The courtier led them into a large, open courtyard. The king sat on embroidered cushions on a platform, shielded from the fierce sun by an umbrella. A large crowd of men, including the two with the menacing swords, stood behind him.

The king stood up. Instantly one hundred onlookers who lined the walls began chanting, "Let the king be strong. Let the king be strong."

The king lifted his hand, and the chanting stopped. Then the king turned his attention to Rowland. The scarlet turban on his head wobbled as he spoke. "I have decided that you must leave our town tomorrow morning. No one may supply you with food after that. There is to be no preaching."

As Rowland's interpreter translated the king's words, a roar of applause was already rising from the crowd.

"You are dismissed," the king snapped at Rowland. "The matter is closed."

Just as Rowland was turning to leave, a man lunged toward him, yelling curses in the name of Allah. Rowland stood transfixed. He had never seen such hatred in a person's eyes. He watched as the man deliberately raised his arm as if to signal something. Rowland waited for mayhem to break out, but nothing happened. The man raised his arm again, but still no one moved. Disgusted, he spat at Rowland and walked away.

As Rowland turned and walked from the king's courtyard, the crowd parted to let him through.

That night two shadowy figures crept into Rowland's tent. Rowland recognized them from the previous night, his first night in Iwo, when they had first come to visit him.

"You are very lucky to be alive," the taller one said. "There is some kind of magic about you."

"What makes you say that?" Rowland asked.

"That man who spat at you and cursed you, he is the head man at the mosque. Early this morning, before you arrived at the palace, he stirred up the people and organized to have you stoned to death as a warning that no other missionaries should disturb Iwo." The man stopped and drew a deep breath before going on. "But when he gave the signal to rush at you, a great fear settled over the people and no one moved. Afterward they said magic held them back, and even the angriest men stepped aside and let you through. You had better leave fast. The king is very scared of you!"

For a brief moment Rowland was tempted to laugh at the thought that the king was very scared of him. Growing up in Kent, England, Rowland had been scared of everything—being alone in the dark, monsters under the bed, ghosts in the graveyard. Back then he could not have begun to imagine himself calmly facing the possibility of his own death in a foreign land. Yes, it had been a strange and fascinating journey that had brought him to the Sudan interior.

Chapter 2

"Be True to Your Principles"

Thirteen-year-old Rowland squirmed in his seat. It was a hot morning, and he was bored with listening to the Latin teacher. He ran his finger over his initials inside the front cover of his grammar book. "R.V.B." Rowland Victor Bingham. Then he took his pen and added, "born December 19, 1872."

Rowland looked up as one of the junior boys ran into the classroom and handed the teacher a note. The teacher frowned and then pointed to Rowland. "To the headmaster's office, on the double," he ordered.

Rowland shut his book and scrambled from his seat, his mind spinning. Why did the headmaster want to see him? Had he done something wrong?

As Rowland walked briskly across the quadrangle, he tried to imagine some deed bad enough to warrant being called out of class, but he could not. He knew he was a good student; he daydreamed a little too much, but he had never been in any sort of trouble. Soon he was standing in front of the headmaster's oak door. He smoothed his mop of thick brown hair, knocked timidly, and waited.

"Come in," came a voice. Rowland pushed the door open and stepped inside. A wave of relief ran through him when he noticed the headmaster had a kindly look on his face.

"Ah, Rowland, lad," the headmaster said. "I have bad news for you. Your father is very ill, and your mother has sent word that you are to go home immediately."

"Right now, sir?" Rowland gulped. "In the middle of Latin class?"

"Yes, yes," the headmaster replied. "You have my permission. Go on home, and be quick about it."

With that Rowland nodded, turned, and rushed out the door. He sprinted to the brick wall that surrounded the school and climbed over it. This was the shortcut home through the back streets of Headcorn, the small village in Kent where he lived. Normally he would have gone the long way around to avoid the foul puddles at the back of the market, but right now he did not care if his shoes got dirty and he was sure his mother would not mind, either.

As he ran down the cobblestone street, Rowland wondered what could have gone wrong. His father was such a big, strong man, one of the strongest men in the village. He owned the local brickyard and sawmill. Maybe something had fallen on him. He was always telling Rowland to watch himself when he was in the timber yard.

Rowland reached the front door of his house just as the kitchen maid stepped outside. "Hurry," she said, pushing him through the door. "Your father is up in his bedroom, and everyone is waiting for you."

Flinging his cap on the table, Rowland took the stairs two at a time. He opened the door to his parents' bedroom. Six pairs of eyes stared at him. They belonged to five of his six brothers and his one sister, and every set of eyes was rimmed with tears.

Mrs. Bingham emerged from the shadows carrying Rowland's youngest brother, three-year-old Guy. "Come in, Rowland. Your father has been waiting for you. He has something he wants to say to all of you."

Rowland walked over to the bed and peered down at his father. His father's eyes were sunken and his skin gray. He smiled weakly at Rowland and then started to speak in a hoarse voice. "Children, I am going to my Savior in heaven. I know I have not lived a perfect life, but as I have lain here, I have asked God to forgive my sins, and I know He has." He stopped for a moment and took a deep, rasping breath. "Now I want each of you to promise me that you will meet me in heaven someday. Will you do that?"

Horace, at fifteen the oldest, was the first to speak. "Yes, Father," he replied, "I promise that one day I will meet you in heaven."

Next to Horace stood Winifred, who made the same promise, as did Rowland's younger brothers, Joseph, Ralph, Harold, and Bill.

Then it was Rowland's turn. He fought back tears as he took his father's hand. "Yes, Papa, I promise I will meet you in heaven when I die."

"Come on, children. It's time to let your father rest now," Rowland heard his mother say.

Numbly Rowland, his older brother Horace following him, walked out of the room, down the stairs, and into the backyard. "How could this happen?" Rowland finally asked his brother as tears spilled down his cheeks.

"The doctor was here when I got home," Horace replied. "He said that it was smallpox."

"Smallpox?" Rowland questioned. "But I thought we had the vaccine so we wouldn't get it."

"Yes, but the doctor said that some people get a regular dose of the disease from the vaccine, and..." he lowered his voice and choked up, "and it can kill them."

"No!" was all Rowland could think to say. It seemed inconceivable to him that his father, who had been so healthy, could be killed by the vaccination he'd had two weeks before.

The two boys sat in silence. Rowland scraped at a rock with the heel of his shoe as they waited for something to happen. They could hear people going in and out the front door. Then, around one o'clock, Rowland watched as his mother drew the curtains in the back rooms. This could mean only one thing:

the house was in mourning. Rowland's father was dead.

The funeral followed soon afterward, and everyone appeared so shocked by the turn of events that no one thought to comfort the children much.

Two weeks later the family was hit with a second blow. Rowland was sitting on the stairs when his mother and the family lawyer walked past him. They were deep in conversation, and neither of them noticed Rowland.

Rowland heard his mother say, "But I can't believe it! Do you mean to tell me that my husband left plenty of money for us, but that it's tied up for the next twenty-one years? Why, all of the children will be raised and out of the house by then! What use will it be to me then?"

"I know; it's most distressing," Rowland heard the lawyer reply. "I wish I had been the one to draw up his will, but it was done before my time. I've looked at it every way I can, but there's nothing legally that can be done. We'll have to put the money into a trust for you, and no one has access to it until 1906. I really wish there were something more I could do for you..." His voice trailed off as he and Mrs. Bingham walked out of earshot. But Rowland had heard enough to alarm him! What was his mother going to do with eight children and no money? And how would it affect him?

Rowland soon found out. Later that evening Mrs. Bingham gathered the oldest four children together and explained the situation to them. She did not have much more light to shed on the subject than Rowland had overheard from the lawyer. Basically, Rowland's father had made some kind of legal mistake in his will and had inadvertently tied up the family money for years to come. Mrs. Bingham explained in a quiet voice that everything was going to be all right and that, no matter what, she would make sure that Rowland and Horace went to college.

Deep in his heart, Rowland doubted this would be possible, and as the next few weeks went by, he realized he would have to get a job to help support the family. Fortunately, even though he was only thirteen years old, he had been in school for ten years. He had started extra young because he'd made such a fuss when Horace went off to school on his fifth birthday that his parents allowed him to start then as well.

With ten years of schooling behind him, Rowland set about finding a position as a student teacher somewhere nearby. He soon found a job in a small village nine miles from the town of Tonbridge. The job paid eighteen pounds a year. That would not be much, especially after he paid for his room and board, but at least his mother would no longer be responsible for feeding him. What little he had left over he would send home to her. In the meantime, Mrs. Bingham decided to move to Tonbridge, where she opened a small general goods store to support the younger children.

Rowland soon learned that being a student teacher was a lot more demanding than being a student. He had to get up at seven o'clock every morning and listen to an hour-long lecture from the headmaster. Then there were prayer and Bible reading by the local clergyman before school started at nine o'clock. Rowland was expected to teach junior classes all day and then mark papers and study for another three or four hours in the evening so that he would know what to teach the following day.

It was not just the work that Rowland found long and difficult. Rowland had a secret he told no one: he was deathly afraid of the dark! At home he had always arranged things so that he did not have to walk alone at night or go up to bed alone, and he always checked under his bed before he got into it. If he heard an unfamiliar noise downstairs, he would stay awake all night waiting for his door handle to turn and someone—or something—to creep into his room. Now that he was a teacher, Rowland had his own room, and he dreaded the day when he would have to go out alone after dark.

That day came soon enough, and much to Rowland's dismay, it came just a few weeks after a murder in the church graveyard that had been the talk of the town. The sexton of the church had gathered his usual group of friends together for a late-night game of cards. There, according to witnesses, as the gambling stakes got higher, tempers got hotter. Eventually an argument broke out and one of the gamblers was stabbed to death. No one was convicted of the crime, and it was said that if you stood by the stone wall overlooking the graveyard in the dead of night, you could hear the rattling of chains—the victim's reminder that no one had yet been locked up for his murder.

Rowland was working late in the classroom one night when the headmaster walked into the room.

"Bingham," the headmaster said, "it's choir practice night, and I left some music books in the church—on the front pew, I think. I need them. Would you mind going and getting them for me? The sexton will give you the keys, a candle, and some matches."

Rowland felt as if he had swallowed a stone. What could he say? The last thing he wanted to do was go into the graveyard at night, but he was too embarrassed to tell the headmaster that he was afraid of the dark.

Before Rowland had a chance to say anything, the headmaster said, "Thank you. Don't be long, will you?" and left the room.

Rowland put down the papers he was grading and looked out the window into the moonless and windy night. Reluctantly he stepped out the door and began the long, lonely walk up over the common that separated the school from the church. His knees shook and his heart pounded as he walked. He tried to whistle, but his mouth was too dry for any sound to come out. Eventually he made it to the sexton's cottage. He thought of asking the sexton to go with him into the church, but once again he was too embarrassed, afraid of being labeled a coward.

The sexton gave Rowland a candle, matches, and a huge key ring. He explained that the longest key, about half the length of Rowland's arm, would open the great oak door of the church. As Rowland turned to go, the sexton shut the cottage door, leaving him alone in the dark once more.

Now the real struggle began. Rowland walked slowly to the gate of the graveyard and peered through the darkness. He could make out the outlines of the tombstones on both sides of the path. He opened the gate and made his way to the church porch, where he tried to strike a match. But the wind caught the small flame and blew it out. Rowland tried desperately three or four more times, but he could not get the match to stay lit. There was nothing to do but forget about the candle.

Rowland fumbled around until he had the key in the lock, then turned it. The door creaked as he pushed it open. The inside of the church was a cavernous black hole in front of him. He stood motionless, fear almost choking him. Suddenly he heard the rattling of chains. Rowland felt his body break out in a cold sweat, and his teeth began to chatter. There was no one to call for help.

Rowland heard more rattling. He wished he could run, but his feet were glued to the floor. Then he heard another sound, a louder one. Boom! And then a second boom. Relief rushed over Rowland as he recognized the sound of the church bell striking the hour. It was nine o'clock. The rattling chains had come from the bell tower!

Rowland waited until all nine tolls were finished, and then he hurriedly lit the candle and walked down the aisle and found the music books on the front pew. As quickly as he could, he scooped up the books and walked back down the aisle, closing and locking the church door behind him. He returned the keys to the sexton before running back to the school.

With great relief Rowland handed over the music books and returned to marking papers. He did not tell anyone the terrible ordeal he had been through. He hoped that one day he would be able to conquer his fears.

The days and weeks sped by in a blur, and Rowland made sure he was never again alone outside in the dark. He tried to keep his spirits up by telling himself that after four years as a student teacher, he would be eligible to become a headmaster—at seventeen years of age.

Rowland could not have foreseen the problem that lay between him and his goal, however. It all started a year after he began as a student teacher. Although the school in which he taught was not owned by any church, it had close ties to the Church of England—the nation's official church—and the local Church of England clergyman was assigned to assist at the school. During Rowland's second year at school, there was a change of clergyman in the village. The new minister was deeply interested in ritual within the church and insisted that many "high church" practices, including the burning of incense and the installation of an elaborate high altar, be introduced in the local parish.

Rowland's mother had often told him his grandfather had been a dissenter. He had been one of the first to refuse to follow the requirements of the official, government-approved church and to worship instead at an "unauthorized" church. And now, as the local Church of England became more formal, Rowland decided that he, too, wanted the simpler form of worship that the dissenters offered. So on Sundays he began walking past the Church of England and on to a small Methodist chapel.

Rowland did not believe that where he went to church was anybody's business but his own—that is, until the new Church of England minister asked to see him after school prayers one morning. Rowland's face dropped as he saw the minister sitting smugly at the back of the hall.

"I have noticed that you have not been in church this last month. What are you doing instead?" the minister asked, stroking his graying beard as he spoke.

Drawing a deep breath, Rowland knew what he was about to say would not be welcome. "I have started attending the Methodist church," he said as calmly as he could. "I find the simplicity of the service much more to my liking."

The minister leaned forward, face darkening like a thundercloud. "You are in a place of public trust," he boomed, "and attending a dissenter church is totally unacceptable. It sets a bad example for your students and cannot be tolerated."

"But I thought I was at liberty to attend church wherever I please," Rowland replied.

The minister grunted. "I know this is not an official church school, but surely you are aware that all the members of the school board are also members of my church. Several of them have urged me to make this matter clear to you. It is their wish, as well as mine, that you stop this nonsense." He looked at Rowland, and his voice softened a little. "Look," he said, "you are young. When you have been about as long as I have, you will understand that sometimes a little compromise is all that is needed. We cannot permit a teacher in this school to lead the students down such a dangerous path. Surely you can understand that? Think of your future. There is a lot at stake here, and no one is asking you to agree with every aspect of the Church of England. It will be enough to see you attend again."

"Thank you for pointing that out," Rowland replied. He wanted to say a lot more, but he did not trust himself. First he wanted to talk to his mother and see what she thought about his dilemma.

"Think about it, lad," the minister said, standing up. "Not that there's much to think about, really. It would seem obvious to me that you need to consider your job first."

"Yes, sir," Rowland muttered as he headed for the side door. He needed some fresh air.

Rowland was stunned as he walked out into the misty morning. What was he supposed to do? That weekend he rode his bicycle home to talk to his mother about the situation. "Be true to your principles," she urged him, even if it meant giving three months' notice and going out to look for another job.

Quite unintentionally, Rowland thus found himself three months away from being unemployed. The bright hopes of one day being a headmaster evaporated like the mist in the surrounding fields. Rowland had no idea what he would do next or how he would make a living.

Chapter 3

"Why Didn't I Go Forward?"

Soon afterward Rowland was back in Tonbridge, this time for the two-week Easter holiday break. Rowland helped his mother out in the store, and when he had time, he tutored his younger sister and brothers, since there was no money for them to go to school.

As Good Friday approached, excitement began to build in Tonbridge. A new group calling itself the Salvation Army had marched into town, waving banners and setting up "barracks" in the Corn Exchange building. The women, who wore navy skirts and jackets and distinctive bonnets, and the men, in their blue serge suits with a brass letter *S* on their collars, seemed to be everywhere. Two days before Good Friday, the town was buzzing with the news that the Salvation Army was going to conduct a funeral service, or a Promotion to Glory, as they called it. Rowland, like many other teenagers in Tonbridge, went to the funeral to see what all the commotion was about. He was astounded. It was unlike any other funeral he had ever been to. As Rowland joined the crowd gathered outside the Corn Exchange, a rowdy brass band belted out drinking tunes as the women sang new Christian words to them. Rowland thought it started out more like a party than a funeral.

As the crowd moved inside and sat down, Rowland felt a strange calm come over him. He sat down and listened as a young, female Salvation Army officer spoke about heaven and hell. His mind drifted back to the promise he had made to his father on his deathbed. Sometimes he had picked up a Bible and read the words of Jesus, trying to work out exactly how he could get to heaven to be reunited with his father, but it wasn't easy. The only passage that seemed to point the way was in Jesus' conversation with Nicodemus, in which Jesus said, "You must be born again." This seemed to Rowland to be an important point, but he was just as puzzled as Nicodemus was as to how to do it. Now, as he craned his neck for a better view of the funeral, his heart raced. Something told him that these people in their blue uniforms might just have the answer.

The following night, Good Friday, March 30, 1887, Rowland announced that he was going to a

Salvation Army meeting. His mother was not happy about it. Attending a dissenter church was one thing, but mixing with the Salvation Army was quite another. The Salvation Army worked with the lowest, most uneducated and despised people in town. Mrs. Bingham told Rowland she hated to think that he had stooped so low as to stand alongside drunkards and street women. For his part, Rowland did not care. He was sure that the Salvation Army held the answer to how he could be born again.

That night Rowland listened intently as one after another chimney sweep, charwoman, and maid stood and told how accepting Jesus Christ into your life was the only way you could have your sins forgiven, and how they had each found peace and joy in their lives by doing so.

Rowland could see it in their faces, which radiated faith and confidence, two things he lacked in his own life. He marveled how in two hours of listening to these simple people he understood more of what Jesus meant about being born again than he had gained in years of sitting in church pews every Sunday.

As the meeting continued, Rowland felt weighed down by thoughts of his own sinfulness. He began to tremble in his seat. It was as if everything the speaker said was directed at him. Finally the speaker invited anyone in the audience who felt that God was tugging at his heart to come forward to the penitent rail. Rowland did not budge. He was too scared to walk to the rail in front of so many people, many of whom were customers he recognized from his mother's shop.

Rowland watched as other people got up out of their seats and walked forward to kneel at the rail, but still he could not do so himself. Eventually he stood, grabbed his cap, and fled from the hall.

A few days later Rowland returned to school to serve out his last eight weeks as a student teacher. As he marked papers and listened to the headmaster, his thoughts were never far from the Salvation Army meeting in Tonbridge. "Why didn't I go forward?" he asked himself a hundred times. "It would have been so easy, and by now I would know that my sins were forgiven and I was going to heaven to be with my father."

After nights of tossing and turning, Rowland reached a decision. The next time he had the opportunity to accept Jesus as his Savior, he was going to do so, no matter how scared he felt!

The opportunity came sooner than expected. Rowland received a letter from a cousin in Grinstead, Sussex, where he had been born and had lived for the first two years of his life. His cousin explained in the letter how he had been "saved" through the Salvation Army, and he invited Rowland to visit him for the Whitsunday holiday. Rowland immediately wrote back, accepting the offer. He also wrote to his mother, suggesting that she, along with the smaller children, come along for a break.

When Rowland arrived in Grinstead, he felt no great excitement. He went to the special holiday program the Salvation Army put on and listened to a converted Jewish man who spoke at the service. But nothing the man said seemed to touch his heart, and by the end of the meeting, Rowland was in a quandary. He had promised himself that the next time he had the opportunity, he would publicly ask Jesus Christ to forgive him of his sins. But now that he was sitting in a seat listening to an altar call, nothing in him wanted to respond to it. All his conviction had evaporated, and his emotions were unmoved.

As Rowland sat wondering what to do, he could not forget the vow he had made. So, without his heart pounding wildly or his knees trembling, as they had on the occasion when he did not go forward, he got up from his seat and made his way to the front and knelt at the penitent rail. Beside him a woman about his mother's age wept, but no tears sprang to Rowland's eyes. Rowland resisted the urge to think of the whole situation as a waste of time and waited for the Jewish man to pray with him. Even when Rowland shut his eyes and repeated a prayer after the man, no emotions welled up within him.

Rowland went back to his cousin's house, glad that he had fulfilled his vow, yet unmoved. However, as the weekend progressed and Rowland attended more Salvation Army meetings, he felt his emotions begin to stir. He felt a tremendous weight of guilt start to roll off him.

Rowland's mother, though, was not at all happy about the changes in her son. While she had understood and even supported Rowland's attendance of a dissenter church, the thought of a member of the family aligning himself with the Salvation Army was too much for her. She told Rowland that the Salvation Army was much too uncouth for a son of hers to belong to. And even though she was now scraping out a living for her family, the Bingham name was a good name, and Rowland ought to think hard before dragging it into a lowly place like the Salvation Army.

Although Rowland listened respectfully to his mother, he had found what he was looking for, and even his mother's disapproval could not shake him from joining in with the Salvation Army. He bought some Salvation Army patches, with their red background and blue border and yellow sun with the motto Blood and Fire emblazoned in the middle, and he sewed them onto his clothes. When his clothes came back from the laundry, he found that his mother had removed the patches.

As far back as he could remember, Rowland had loved to play the autoharp. Now he often played hymns on street corners, hoping to strike up a conversation about Christ with a passerby. When his family heard about this, they were horrified, but Rowland was undaunted. When his final three months of teaching were over, he gladly left the school and went home to share the "good news" with his mother, sister, and brothers. Horace had left home by now, and thirteen-year-old Joseph had just left to join the navy, leaving five children in the house.

On his first night living back home, Rowland found it difficult to sleep. He knew he had to find a way to talk to his family about the gospel, but his mother was so against the Salvation Army that he did not know how to do it without upsetting her further. Finally, just as the clock struck three in the morning, he decided on a plan. At breakfast he would ask if he could read the Bible and pray before everyone set about the day's tasks.

Rowland's plan did not get off to a good start. In the morning he learned that his mother was sick in bed and would not be getting up until later. Still, Rowland was determined to do something. He put his small Bible in his pocket and prepared a breakfast tray for his mother. He could feel his heart thumping as he climbed the stairs and knocked on her door. He placed the tray on the bed, poured tea for his mother, and then paced the floor trying to get up the courage to speak.

Finally the words came. "Mother, I feel I should read to you this morning," Rowland said as he quickly opened his Bible and started reading from the Gospel of John. Since his mother did not tell him to stop, Rowland read a whole chapter. When he was finished, he walked out of the bedroom with a tremendous sense of relief. He had overcome his fear and done what he had set out to do.

The joy Rowland felt did not carry over to the next morning, however, when his mother was better. This time Rowland knew that he needed to read the Bible in front of the entire family. Since he was sure that his brothers and sister would not want to hang around for a Bible reading, as soon as they were all eating their porridge, he slipped into the hallway to pray for the courage to read aloud to them. Once again his heart beat furiously, but he knew what he had to do. He opened his Bible and pushed open the dining room door, and without going in, he started to read. The children were quiet for a moment, and then they began to giggle and carry on talking. Rowland did not care. He felt sure he was doing what God wanted him to do, and that was all that mattered.

The next morning Rowland followed the same procedure. Again his brothers and sister kept talking over him, as they continued to do every day for a week. Then, on the eighth day, Rowland faced an even greater challenge. A friend of his mother's had come to stay, and she, too, sat at the breakfast table. Rowland knew she would think that his little morning ritual was very strange, but by now he did not care. He stood at the door and read from his Bible.

Rowland was most surprised when the woman glared at the children in such a way as to quiet them down so that everyone could hear. Three days after the visitor's arrival, Rowland found himself alone with her in the living room. The fire in the grate glowed golden orange as the two sat in silence. Then the woman unexpectedly asked, "Rowland, what makes you read that way in the mornings?"

Rowland took a deep breath and answered her as plainly as he could, telling her of the joy he had found when he asked Jesus Christ to forgive his sins and change his life. He then sat stunned as the woman burst into tears and said, "Do you think He would save me?"

"Well, I think He would," Rowland stuttered. It had never occurred to him that someone else might be saved though his words!

"Then please tell me what to do. I have been wanting to find my way to God for so long."

Rowland led the woman in a very simple prayer; he was too shocked to think of anything fancy to say. As he thought about the incident later, Rowland was overjoyed to think that God could use a fifteen-year-old boy in his own home.

Things at home were about to take a turn for the worse for Rowland. The problem was tobacco. Since Rowland was having difficulty finding another job, he helped out in his mother's store, where brightly colored tins of tobacco lined the top shelf. This presented him with a dilemma, for he no longer believed it was right for a Christian to sell tobacco, and especially not to the same young boys who came to inquiry meetings at the Salvation Army. That was where Rowland spent all his spare time, and it bothered him that the boys he talked to about how God could help them to change their bad habits were the same boys he sold tobacco to.

Eventually Rowland summoned up the courage to tell his mother he could no longer sell tobacco. In reply she told him that tobacco was one of the staple items she sold and that the store would not make enough profit to support them if she did not sell it. Rowland and his mother had reached an impasse. She insisted he sell tobacco, and his conscience would not let him do it.

Rowland prayed about the situation for several weeks until he read an advertisement for a ship that was taking emigrants to Canada. Something stirred within Rowland as he read the advertisement. Although he knew it was a drastic way out of his situation, he felt sure that God wanted him to leave England and venture out on his own. When he shared his plan with his mother, he did not tell her he was leaving over the tobacco issue. He did not want her to think her stand had driven him out of the house.

Finally the day arrived, and sixteen-year-old Rowland Bingham swung a knapsack over his shoulder and boarded a train for London. It was hard to leave his family, but he was confident that Winifred and Ralph were old enough to be useful to their mother. Once he arrived at Waterloo Station in London, he found a cart to take him to the dock. As he looked up at the steamship on which he had bought a cheap ticket, he wondered what his life would be like across the Atlantic Ocean in Halifax, Nova Scotia, Canada.

Chapter 4

A Continent in Darkness Haunted Him

Although Rowland was only sixteen years old, traveling across the Atlantic made him feel grown up. There was no one now to give him advice or to help him out of difficult situations; he was on his own. While on board the steamer, Rowland decided to use his newfound independence and hold Sunday services in the dining room. During these services he had to shout to make himself heard above the sound of the ocean crashing against the hull of the ship, but Rowland did not mind.

Rowland was very encouraged when he learned that a passenger who had been lying sick in his bunk had heard him preaching at the top of his lungs and been converted through the message. From then on, preaching and running small Bible studies on the ship kept Rowland busy until, on March 31, 1889, the steamer tied up alongside the dock in Halifax. It was one year and one day since Rowland had knelt at the penitent rail at the Salvation Army meeting in Grinstead.

Rowland soon found a job as a farm laborer nine miles east of Halifax. This meant that he had to walk that distance and back each Sunday to church in the city, often carrying his autoharp, but Rowland did not mind. He enjoyed the exercise, and soon found a Salvation Army corps to join. Each Sunday after the meeting, he and several other young men spent the afternoon preaching and singing on street corners.

After a year in Halifax, Rowland moved to Toronto to find more fulfilling work. Once again he linked up with the Salvation Army, and after he found a job as a clerk, he spent his spare time street preaching and passing out gospel tracts and literature. It was on one of these occasions that something happened that would alter the direction of his life.

Rowland was standing on a street corner selling copies of the Salvation Army's magazine *War Cry* when a middle-aged man stopped in front of him. "Will you buy a *War Cry*, sir?" Rowland asked.

The man looked at Rowland. "Tell me how old you are, lad."

"Eighteen," Rowland replied.

"And are you saved?"

"Yes, sir, three years now," Rowland said.

"How do you know you are saved?"

Since Rowland sensed that the man was not trying to draw him into an argument, he told him how he had felt relieved when he asked Jesus Christ to take away his sins, and how the Bible said that a man could be born again. As he spoke, Rowland was painfully aware of fumbling over the ideas he was trying to present. When he was finished, the man offered his hand to Rowland.

"My name is John Salmon," he said, "and I commend you on the work you are doing. You appear to have a lot of enthusiasm. Perhaps one day you will consider a little more formal training so that you can go on in your Christian work." He then reached into his pocket and pulled out a penny to buy a copy of *War Cry.*

The whole encounter had taken less than five minutes, but its impact on Rowland was undeniable. Rowland knew that John Salmon was a legendary preacher in Toronto and the "father" of the Christian and Missionary Alliance Church in Canada. If Mr. Salmon thought he needed more training, Rowland was ready to consider it. However, he did not know how to go about getting such training. His life was already filled with his job and his street work for the Salvation Army.

A year later Rowland was preaching at a street meeting when he spotted John Salmon at the back of the crowd. When he finished preaching, Rowland approached the pastor.

"How are things going for you, lad?" Mr. Salmon asked.

"Fine, thank you, sir," Rowland politely replied.

"I see you are still working on the streets. Did you manage to get any more training?"

Rowland shook his head. "No," he replied, "but I would like to."

"You would, would you?" John Salmon said. "Let me think. I am in need of an assistant right now, what with trying to get Bethany Chapel up and running. Would you consider coming to live with my family? I could give you Bible instruction, and you could earn your keep by being my pastoral assistant."

Rowland hardly knew what to say. *The* Reverend Salmon was offering to tutor him in Bible study and trust him to be his assistant! "Yes, I would like that," Rowland blurted out.

The year and a half that Rowland spent serving as John Salmon's assistant was busy and stretching. Soon after taking the position, Rowland handed in his resignation as a Salvation Army officer. And although he missed the Army, he did not regret leaving. He had plenty of new opportunities to share his faith and so much to learn.

One evening in May 1893, Rowland was sharing a testimony at Bethany Chapel. When the service was over, an elderly woman approached him. "Young man," she said in a thick Scottish brogue, "I listened to every word you said, and I would like to invite you to come fellowship with me over lunch tomorrow."

"Thank you. That is very kind of you. Do you live far from here?" Rowland inquired.

"Just around the corner. My name is Mrs. Gowans," the woman said, smiling. "I have two children serving the Lord overseas, and I would like to tell you about them."

Mrs. Gowans wrote her address down, and the following day Rowland arrived for lunch. Mr. Gowans and several teenage children joined them for the kind of home-cooked dinner that reminded Rowland of his own mother's cooking. When the dishes were cleared away, Mrs. Gowans invited Rowland to sit in the front room, where she pulled two framed photographs from the mantel and showed them to Rowland.

"This is our Annie," Mrs. Gowans said proudly. "God called her to China as a missionary two years ago. She is working with abandoned children there now and preaching in the villages."

Rowland was very impressed as he looked at the photo of a smiling young woman. Then Mrs. Gowans handed him the second photo. "This is Walter. He's twenty-five years old," she said. "He is on his way to England at the moment. He is going there to raise interest for his mission to Africa, and then he is taking a ship to that dark land."

"Which mission agency is he going there with?" Rowland asked.

Mrs. Gowans shook her head. "He's not going with any of them. Not that he didn't want to. He applied to many of them in North America, but he could not find one that was prepared to send him to such a dangerous place. So he's gone off to England to see if some organization there will take him on." She paused and put the photo back on the mantel. "Do you know much about Africa, Mr. Bingham?" she asked.

"Not a lot," Rowland confessed.

"Let me tell you a little about it," Mrs. Gowans said, pouring a cup of tea for Rowland and handing it to him. "My son feels particularly called to the Sudan, a great expanse of land south of the Sahara Desert and bounded on the west by the Niger River and on the east by the Nile. In this belt of land stretching some twenty-five hundred miles across Africa live ninety million people. And do you know what, Mr. Bingham?"

Rowland gave her a blank stare. This little Scottish woman knew her geography!

"There is not one missionary in all of the Sudan, and neither is there one Christian," Mrs. Gowans said, her voice rising to a crescendo.

"Not one?" Rowland questioned.

"Not one. The only missionaries live along the coast and do not venture inland. Yet the people of the Sudan live in darkness, with no knowledge of the gospel. In the north they are Muslims, and in the south, pagans locked in superstition and fear. Dark, horrible things happen there. For instance, twins are considered a bad omen. After their birth, their heads are smashed together by the witch doctor to kill them, and their bodies are left for wild animals to eat. The mother is often murdered, too, for carrying such a curse to the village. Many of these people are also cannibals. They cook and eat their enemies and then use their bleached skulls to decorate their houses. And the Muslim leaders in the north are no better. They send their armies south to attack villages and capture healthy young people, who are chained together and marched north to be used as slaves." Mrs. Gowans paused for dramatic effect. "This is the dark place God is calling my son to, but someone must bring the light of Christ to them."

Rowland didn't quite know what to say in response. He had never heard the needs of a place presented so passionately. Indeed, he was so spellbound by what Mrs. Gowans had to say that he hadn't even taken a sip of his tea, which was now lukewarm in the cup.

Before Rowland found the words to respond, Mrs. Gowans spoke again. "What about you, Mr. Bingham? Are you prepared to join my son in his mission if God calls you to do so?"

Again Rowland didn't know quite what to say. It was a question he had not been expecting.

That night as Rowland lay in bed, he could not get the picture of Walter Gowans out of his mind, or the words of Walter's mother, for that matter: "Are you prepared to join my son in his mission if God calls you to do so?" The words echoed over and over. Rowland tried to counteract them with other thoughts. There was plenty of work to be done in Canada, for instance, and what would Reverend Salmon do without an assistant? It would be hard to train another assistant who could read his handwriting and who knew the inner workings of his intricate filing system. But nothing helped. The thought of a continent in darkness haunted Rowland, and by morning he had made up his mind: he was going right back to Mrs. Gowans's house to find out where Walter was staying in England, and then he was going to go and join him in Africa! Mrs. Gowans was overjoyed at the news. She furnished Rowland with all the information he would need to find Walter in England.

As he left the Gowans's house, the enormity of what he had just done settled over Rowland. At twenty years of age, he had committed himself to serving in Africa—the white man's grave, as it was so often called because of the huge number of deaths of Europeans who had gone there, mostly from tropical diseases.

But while Rowland might have committed to go to Africa, he had less than ten dollars to his name. It wasn't even enough to get to London, much less Africa.

Lacking money for his passage, Rowland went to visit a Christian family he had become friendly with. James and Elizabeth Blair had five sons, and a daughter around Rowland's age. Once, months before, James Blair had told Rowland that if he ever wanted to be a missionary, he would gladly help support him. But now that he was actually in the Blair home, Rowland was too scared to bring the subject up. On his last morning, it was James who finally brought up the issue over breakfast.

"I haven't forgotten my promise to you several months ago," he began. "However, a man borrowed a large sum from me last week. I have little ready cash available at the moment, but I shall empty my bank account and give you all I have. And if you need more, I shall borrow it and give it to you."

"No. No. I won't think of your having to borrow money on my behalf. But if you feel led to give me what is in your account, that would be most generous," Rowland said.

After breakfast the two men went into town, where James withdrew the last $125 from his bank account and handed it to Rowland.

With some of the money, Rowland booked passage to England on a steamer leaving from New York City. He left for New York right away. While waiting in New York for the ship to depart, Rowland met another young man named Tom Kent. As the two of them talked, Rowland discovered that Tom had been a college friend of Walter Gowans when he was attending the Reverend A. B. Simpson's Missionary Institute in New York City. Rowland gave Tom an enthusiastic update on Walter's mission, and before the conversation was over, Tom asked if he could go along.

Rowland was overjoyed at this turn of events, though he was not sure what Walter would say, and there was no time to ask him. It would take too long for a letter to get across the Atlantic Ocean to England and back with a reply. Instead, Rowland helped Tom settle up his affairs before the two of them set sail for England. They departed exactly two weeks after Rowland had spoken to Mrs. Gowans in her house.

The spring crossing of the Atlantic Ocean aboard the SS *Umbria* was surprisingly calm. Four years had passed since Rowland left England for Canada, and he looked forward to visiting his family one last time before heading to Africa.

Rowland enjoyed Tom's company on the trip. The two of them prayed together each morning and held Bible studies in their cabin in the evening. At twenty-three, Tom was three years older than Rowland, and Rowland admired his quiet faith and Bible knowledge.

When the *Umbria* finally docked in Liverpool, England, in mid-June 1893, a letter from Walter Gowans was waiting for Rowland. Rowland ripped it open and began to read.

> My Dear Brother Bingham,
>
> On looking over your letter last night I find that just about this time you will have arrived in England, that is of course calculating from the dates you gave me in your letter. Well my brother I rejoice exceedingly and praise God for the way in which He has led you especially at this juncture and in regard to this great work....
>
> On arriving in Scotland I lost no time before ascertaining whether there was any prospect of cooperation in the work from that quarter and finding none came on straightway to London. But in London also I found nothing but indifference, halfheartedness and opposition, oh! My brother it is the same everywhere, sleeping societies, sleeping Christians, sleeping church! Yes, a dead church but Blessed be God we have a "living" Christ!

Rowland stopped reading for a moment. This was not the kind of news he had been hoping for. He sighed and read on.

> My brother, one staggers to think of the immensity of our undertaking; ninety millions without Christ, the great Sudan untouched. One might well stagger and ask who is sufficient for these things? But our sufficiency is of God. He is able and He can do all things through Christ which strengtheneth us and we will.

The letter went on to give the address where Walter was staying and invited Rowland to come there as soon as his luggage was unloaded.

During the next few hours, Rowland reread the letter several times. It was true, the three of them were about to undertake a mission that seemed impossible, yet he reminded himself that even the biggest oak tree comes from the smallest acorn. If they continued to follow God, surely things would go well for them all. Rowland had no idea how much such simple faith would be tested in the months to come.

Chapter 5

"You Will Never See the Sudan"

Nearly five months later, on November 4, 1893, Walter Gowans, Tom Kent, and Rowland Bingham stood on the aft deck of a ship watching the coastline of England slip from view. They were finally on their way to Africa! Although it should have been a wonderful moment for Rowland, he was filled with conflicting thoughts. For one thing, they had not been able to find a single missionary board in Great Britain that would take up their cause. Rowland understood why. Last spring the Church of England's Church Missionary Society had sent six promising men, including a bishop, up the Niger River into the central Sudan. Now four of them lay in graves on the border of that immense territory.

Without a mission board behind them, the men had no one but Mrs. Gowans to keep churches updated on their news and prayer requests. Rowland smiled to himself. *If we have to have a one-woman missionary board, there is no woman I would rather have behind me than Mrs. Gowans,* he thought. *She has enough enthusiasm and vision to do the work of ten others.*

Because the men had not found a mission board in England willing to take them on, Walter had come up with a name for the three of them. They would call themselves the Sudan Interior Mission (SIM for short), and Walter's mother would be their entire mission board. Rowland liked the name; it had a no-nonsense ring to it.

The men were grateful that individual Christians had given them enough money to pay all their passages from Liverpool to Lagos, West Africa. And they still had 150 pounds with which to journey from Lagos inland into the Sudan.

When the last rocky outcrop of the English coast slipped over the horizon, Rowland went below deck and set up things in his cabin. He pulled out two photographs and placed them on the rail beside his bunk. The first was of his mother. It had been wonderful to see her and his brothers and sister again. His mother was doing better in the shop now, and she seemed reconciled to Rowland's striking out as a missionary. The other photo was of the three young men. Rowland took a long look at it. The men sat stiffly, Walter with his distinguished moustache and holding a Bible, Tom with his arms crossed in quiet determination, and Rowland on the right, wearing his bow tie and with a slight smile on his oval, boyish face.

What lies in store for us? Rowland thought as he studied the faces. *Will we be dead by this time next month, or next year? Or will we be on a boat home, sick and unable to carry on?* Rowland had no answers to these questions. But he did know one thing: all three of them believed that God had called them to Africa.

It took Rowland a few days to get used to the rolling of the ship. Once he had adjusted, he enjoyed standing on deck talking to the captain, an educated man who liked to tell mariner's tales. The captain explained to Rowland that up until thirty years ago, Lagos had been a notorious pirate port. British ships dared not drop anchor there for fear of being boarded and robbed. In 1861 the king of Lagos had been caught up in local wars, and to gain protection from the British Empire, he had ceded his island domain and a strip along the mainland to Queen Victoria. In return the queen promised that the Royal Navy would protect him. Now, without the pirates, Lagos had become the busiest port in Africa.

There were other tales, too, of the captain's friends who had ventured inland in search of trading goods and witnessed cannibal ceremonies and seen large bands of slaves shackled together and being driven north. In 1833 Britain had banned slavery in its territories, but there was still a thriving slave trade within Africa. The more Rowland heard of it, the more he prayed that God would use the three of them to make an impact on this vast land.

The ship rounded Cape Verde and headed east parallel to the equator. The three young missionaries were constantly on deck now, watching as the rolling hills of the cape swept by. It was only a matter of days now before they reached Lagos!

The first signs that the ship was reaching Lagos were the small, pointed canoes laden with fishing nets. Next came more canoes, this time bearing bunches of bananas and baskets of cocoa beans for barter. As Rowland peered over the side at the traders, he was thrilled. He and his two companions had made it to Africa. Now all they had to do was reach the Sudan interior.

The captain explained that since the ship was too large to sail into the harbor at Lagos and berth, everything going ashore, including the passengers, would have to be off-loaded into smaller boats called lighters.

The lighter carrying the three young missionaries edged its way around several marshy islands, past a sandbar, and into a large palm tree–lined lagoon. Lagos was situated on the western edge of the lagoon. As the boat got closer to the dock, Rowland could see that it was alive with activity. The women were wrapped in brightly colored cloth, the men wore billowing embroidered robes, and babies bobbed up and down on their mothers' backs. Hundreds of barrels stacked five high stood at one end of the dock, with crates of live, cackling hens in front of them.

Suddenly the lighter lurched, and ropes were thrown up and secured around the dock pilings. One by one the passengers climbed up and onto the dock. Soon the three young men were all standing on the dock surrounded by their cabin trunks and bags.

Rowland and Tom decided to stay with the baggage while Walter went in search of rooms to rent. As they waited, people went about their daily business, paying no attention to Rowland and Tom. Women sold bags of peanuts and pots of yams floating in oil. Men, their muscles gleaming with sweat, rolled barrels onto boats, while children wove in and out between them. Rowland wondered how they found the energy for such work in the oppressive heat that was sapping the strength from him as he stood still.

An hour later Walter returned with a grin on his face. "Things have gone famously," he said. "I found a house for rent, and would you believe it, the man who owns it also owns this dock, so he is sending his men to carry our baggage and help us through customs."

"Thank God," Rowland said. The first hurdle of finding a place to stay appeared to be solved.

The process of clearing customs went surprisingly fast with the help of the local men. The three missionaries found the house they had rented to be small but adequate, since they did not have many possessions to fill it.

On December 7, 1893, three days after the men arrived in Lagos, a messenger arrived at their door with an invitation to dine with the superintendent of the Methodist mission. Rowland was eager to meet another missionary. He looked forward to hearing the superintendent's insights on the Sudan and learning how they should go about getting inland, but he was in for a shock.

No sooner had they all sat down to dinner than the superintendent shook his head. "Young men," he said, "I would be neglecting my duty if I did not tell you that you are on a fool's errand. You will never see the Sudan." He looked sternly at each of them, and then to emphasize his warning, he pointed his fork at them and added, "Your children will never see the Sudan; your grandchildren might." He reached for another slice of beef and continued. "Such a waste. I learned of another party of six missionaries who landed in Lagos today and have set their sights on the lower Niger. No doubt they will perish or retreat as well. Where exactly are you headed, anyway?"

"We plan to make it to Bida and set up a work there," Walter replied.

"Pure fantasy," the superintendent said. "Don't waste your lives."

Rowland wanted desperately to think of some fact to contradict the superintendent, but what could he say? Everyone who knew of the conditions in the Sudan interior had predicted more or less the same fate for them. Instead, he remembered the biography he had read aboard ship. It was of David Livingstone, the great missionary explorer who had spent thirty-two years in Africa. Livingstone, who had died twenty years before, had met with a lot of discouragement too, and his response was, "I will open up central Africa to the gospel, or I will die in the attempt!" As he choked down the rest of his dinner, Rowland made a silent promise that he, too, would either succeed in his mission or die trying.

The superintendent's words did not discourage any of the three young men for long, though his warning did cause them to pray even harder. In fact, the men decided to spend a week in prayer for their mission.

Although none of the men had admitted it to the superintendent, they realized that they did not have enough money to mount a successful inland trip. At the end of their week of prayer, they felt they should sort through their belongings and sell anything that was not essential. Since the sun rose and set at almost exactly the same time every day and was high above their heads at noon, they reasoned they no longer needed their pocket watches to tell time. They also sold the small canvas boat they had brought, along with extra sets of clothing. They pooled their profits and decided to share everything according to who needed it, just as the disciples had done after the Day of Pentecost.

Next they examined their food budget and decided to stop buying meat and bread, living instead on corn mix. The locals made this into a porridge that they ate with palm oil. At first Rowland gagged when he ate the mixture, but gradually his body adjusted to it. The change in diet reduced their living expenses to about two pennies a day each. However, even selling their belongings and eating frugally did not raise as much money as they had hoped, and the three of them found themselves praying more for God's provision.

The answer to their prayers came from the humblest of quarters. While in England they had stayed with a rich family and had talked with the housemaid, a woman named Mary Jones. When mail finally arrived from England, it contained a letter from Mary. As Rowland opened the letter, a bank draft for five hundred pounds floated out.

Rowland could scarcely believe it! A maid sending them such a huge sum. He quickly read the letter that came with the money. Mary wrote that she had received a legacy of three hundred pounds from a distant relative and felt that God wanted her to send the entire amount to the three young missionaries. When her mistress heard of her sacrifice, she added one hundred pounds more, and various others had contributed too, until the total reached five hundred pounds.

Now the men had plenty of money for all three of them to go inland, and they hoped to be on their way before Christmas. However, the dreaded disease malaria struck. Rowland was the first to fall ill. On December 19, his twenty-first birthday, his head throbbed, and his body felt like it was on fire. By Christmas Day he was so sick that Tom and Walter borrowed a stretcher and carried him to the Church Missionary Society compound, which had a small hospital attached to it. As Rowland lay semiconscious, he heard his friends praying that he would live to see the new year.

Sometime later Rowland was vaguely aware that he had a visitor—Bishop Hill, one of the two survivors of the Church Missionary Society's foray up the Niger River. Bishop Hill had heard that Rowland was sick and came to pray for him. Rowland could not even open his mouth to thank the bishop for his concern, but the prayers of a fellow missionary meant a lot to him.

Just after New Year's Day, the doctor informed Rowland that the worst was behind him and that he was on the road to recovery. This was hard for Rowland to believe, since every bone in his body ached and he was constantly lathered in sweat. Still, he was discharged from the hospital and into the care of Tom and Walter.

No sooner had Rowland returned to their little rented house than he got word that Bishop Hill and his wife had both suddenly taken ill and died. Rowland wondered whether the gloomy predictions that no white men could survive long in the Sudan might be true.

It was three weeks before Rowland was able to shuffle around the house, but he was still very weak and tired easily. This fact made what could have been a difficult decision easier. The three men had decided that one of them should stay behind in or around Lagos, keeping a home base and sending out more supplies as they were needed. This job fell to Rowland, since he was too weak to travel anyway. Rowland was disappointed that he would not be going with the other two men, but he understood why he had been selected to stay behind.

The three missionaries used some of the money that Mary Jones had sent to buy goods to barter with. They had been told that in the interior their money was useless. The only currency exchanged was the cowrie, a small shell worth one hundredth of a cent. Its tiny value meant that taking cowrie shells along to buy things with was totally impractical. Instead, other missionaries who lived along the coast advised the men to buy bolts of cotton fabric and knives and scissors to take with them to barter for the goods they needed as they made their way inland.

Since they would have to set up their own camp at night, they also needed strong men to carry their equipment and help them set things up. There was no shortage of strong men, but few of them were willing to venture inland to Bida for any price. They told the men that if they did so, raiding parties from the north would round them up and march them inland to be sold as slaves.

Eventually, though, the missionaries found enough men willing to accompany them, and on February 23, 1894, Rowland wrote in his journal, "Walter and Tom left Lagos for Sudan." He wrote no more that day. What could he say? All three of them knew what a treacherous journey lay ahead. And to make matters worse, they had learned that of the party of six missionaries that had landed in Lagos soon after them, four were already dead and one was on his way home because of illness. Only one of them was still pressing inland. With this news on his mind, Rowland bid his friends farewell and promised to pray for them each day.

Chapter 6

Death Sentence

Rowland returned to the empty house. He ate his dinner of cold porridge and mangos alone and prayed that his friends would make it to Bida. One week went by, and then two. A British merchant offered Rowland a part-time bookkeeping job. The pay was not much, but it came with a place to stay. Rowland took the job to save money, since the funds were beginning to run low by now and he had no idea when to expect Walter and Tom back.

Once he had moved in with the merchant, Rowland plotted his own shorter trips into the interior. He made sure he was never away for more than a few days at a time in case his two friends showed up or sent a message asking for something to be sent to them.

The first trip Rowland planned was to Iwo, about four days' journey northwest of Lagos. After hiring several porters and a Christian native to act as his interpreter, Rowland set out.

Even with others carrying his belongings, Rowland was stunned at how grueling the travel was. Not only was the weather oppressively hot, but the tracks were overgrown and winding. And everyone was constantly on the lookout for deadly snakes in the grass and crocodiles in the rivers.

As the men walked the trail north, Rowland's interpreter explained that since Iwo was a Muslim town, the first thing Rowland should do upon his arrival there was to go to the king of the city, pay his respects, and ask for permission to preach and teach in the town. Without that permission, none of the people in the town would dare to listen to what he had to say and he could be thrown in jail.

When they arrived at the palace at Iwo, that is what Rowland did. He was astonished at the wealth the king surrounded himself with. Decorations made of beaten gold hung on the walls, and the king's silver walking stick was ornately carved. It was quite a contrast to the honeycomb of mud huts Rowland had seen while walking on the outskirts of the city.

The king did not look happy to see Rowland, but he told him to come back in the morning to hear his decree on preaching the gospel in Iwo. Rowland and his small entourage then pitched their tents outside the city and waited for morning.

Soon after dark, Rowland saw two shadowy figures outside his tent. His heart beat like a drum, but he summoned his courage and scanned the darkness. Sure enough, two sets of eyes peered back at him. Two men motioned that they wanted to come inside, and Rowland stepped aside to let them in. When the men said something Rowland could not understand, he called for his interpreter.

"Do not tell the king we have come. He would be very angry with us, but we had to see for ourselves that a man with peeled skin has come to Iwo." Rowland's interpreter translated their words to English and added that they used the term *peeled skin* because they thought that white people had peeled off the black layer of their skin.

"Why do they want to see me?" Rowland asked, wondering why two men would risk the ire of their master to come and talk to him.

The two slaves looked at each other, and then the younger of the two spoke. "Because we have heard that where the peeled skinned ones come, the slaves are set free. Is this true? Are we free now?"

Rowland shook his head. He wished he had the power to set all the slaves free, but he did not. He did, however, have a message that would make them free in their hearts, and he prayed he would be given permission to preach that message the next day. Perhaps these two men would even respond to it.

In the morning Rowland's hopes were dashed. He and his interpreter once again set out for the palace, but rather than give him permission to preach, the king ordered Rowland to leave the town. If not for God's protection, the head man of Iwo's mosque would have had his way and Rowland would have been stoned to death by a mob of angry townspeople.

That night, which the king had declared would have to be Rowland's last night in Iwo, the two slaves returned to Rowland's tent. They reported that the townspeople were saying that magic had protected Rowland. But Rowland recalled the Bible verse he had quoted earlier in the day: "I am with thee, and no man shall set on thee to hurt thee."

"It is not magic, my friends," Rowland told the visitors. "It is the hand of God. I have come to tell you good news, and He is the one who gave me protection. Tell your friends that there is a powerful God who loves them very much, and that one day more men with white skin will come to tell them about Him."

The following morning Rowland set out for Lagos again. He was disappointed that he could not preach in Iwo, but he was heartened that God had protected him in the midst of great trouble. He imagined he felt a bit like Daniel must have felt when he walked out of the lions' den.

Rowland arrived back in Lagos just in time. On July 9 he received a hand-delivered letter saying that Tom was on his way back to the city for more supplies and that Walter was pressing on slowly northward.

The letter did not prepare Rowland for the shock of seeing Tom in person four days later. Tom staggered into town, his body covered from head to foot with oozing boils and his temperature soaring.

Rowland put his friend to bed immediately and went to fetch a doctor. Tom had malaria. Thankfully, it was not a fatal case, and Tom made a good recovery. He was strong enough to sit up in bed and recount some of the problems the missionary duo had encountered on the trip north.

"Keeping the native carriers working was the hardest thing of all," Tom confided. "Sometimes I despaired, thinking that we would have to abandon all of our trading goods and walk on alone."

"Why?" Rowland asked. "They seemed an eager lot."

Tom sighed. "Eager! Cunning is more like it. They would carry our goods for about twenty miles, into the middle of nowhere, and then every man would put down his load, and their leader would say, 'White man, we cannot go any farther unless you double our pay.' What could we do? If we doubled their pay, they would pull the same trick next week and want it doubled again."

"What did you do?" Rowland asked.

"We just had to wait them out. Walter was great at it. He would thank them for bringing us to such a beautiful spot and tell them that we would settle right there for a few weeks and that they were not needed anymore. Then they would go into the nearest village, and a week later, when their pay was all spent, they would come back to us and offer to go on. Then, when they had some pay owed them, they would repeat the whole process. It took six weeks for us to cover six days of traveling. You have no idea how frustrating it was, especially in the heat, and our supplies were running out too."

On August 29, 1894, a month and a half after arriving in Lagos, Tom announced that he was well enough to head north to join Walter once again. He took a fresh lot of supplies with him and set out.

Rowland stayed behind, working part-time and taking short preaching trips when he could. He eagerly awaited news from Tom, but he never heard from him again.

Within weeks Rowland received a note stating that Tom had made it as far as Bida, where he'd had a relapse of malaria. This time there were no doctors, though two white missionaries who were trekking through the area did care for him as best they could. Sadly, there was not much they could do for Tom, who became unconscious and died. He was buried within hours, and his belongings were bundled up to be sent on to Walter.

Rowland read the letter three or four times, but it was hard for him to grasp its meaning. Was Tom really dead? Tom had left Lagos with such promise and determination. Rowland wondered why God had allowed Tom to die while sparing him from being stoned to death in Iwo. It did not make sense to him at all. To make matters worse, Rowland had the painful task of writing to Tom's parents to tell them of their son's death. *Will someone be writing to my mother with the same news soon?* he asked himself as he wrote.

Gloomy days followed, and then a month later another tragedy rocked Rowland's faith. It came in the form of another letter, this time written by Walter Gowans's guide, a native Christian named Tom Coffee. As Rowland scanned the letter, a sentence jumped out at him. "I am very sorry to inform you that Mr. Gowans was dead, of bellyache…" Rowland slumped in his chair; his mind went numb as he read the words. How could it be? First Tom Kent, and now Walter Gowans—both dead.

It was two weeks before Rowland learned the details of Walter's death. Walter became ill soon after Tom left to return to Lagos for more supplies, and he took refuge in a small town while awaiting Tom's return. But the army of a slave-raiding king from the north surrounded the town. And while the townspeople fought valiantly against them, the army eventually starved them into submission, capturing and enslaving the entire population. Seeing that he had captured a white man, the king decided to let Walter go free but not before taking everything he had. With his health failing, Walter stumbled on to the town of Zaria, where he met three other white men on a scientific expedition to the interior. When they saw how sick Walter was, they arranged for him to be taken back to Lagos, but two days later, on November 17, 1894, in the town of Girku, on his way back to the coast, Walter died. His helper, Tom Coffee, buried Walter's body in a nearby cornfield.

Rowland was devastated by the two deaths. It all seemed so senseless, and the words of the superintendent of the Methodist mission echoed in his mind: "You will never see the Sudan." Should they have listened to his advice? Was it foolhardy to think that missionaries could ever penetrate the Sudan interior?

Rowland would have liked to discuss these questions with someone, but both his companions were dead. He was the lone surviving member of the Sudan Interior Mission, and he did not know what to do. It seemed futile to set out for the interior without any kind of support system. Yet he hated the thought of returning to England or Canada, where the whole enterprise was bound to be branded a failure.

For the next five months, Rowland preached around Lagos while he wrestled with his future and the future of the one-man mission he had inherited. Finally, in early April 1895, he decided to return to Canada. He hoped to rouse support at home for SIM and bring new missionaries back with him. But as he packed up his few belongings, along with Walter's journal and pen, Rowland wondered how he would ever find anyone to come back with him. Who would volunteer for a death sentence?

Chapter 7

It Would Have Been Easier to Die in Africa

During the voyage home, Rowland had a lot of time to think, more time than he wanted. Not an hour passed that he did not think about Walter and Tom. These men's deaths had shaken his faith to its foundation. Rowland had gone to Africa trusting in God's promises of health and healing, and yet he had left two of the most faithful Christians he knew buried in the Sudan. *Did the promises of God fail?* he asked himself over and over. Why should those who were the most anxious to carry out the Lord's command to take the gospel to the millions in darkness be the ones cut off at the beginning of their mission?

Yet as Rowland pondered these things, he found solace in Walter's journal. Often in the evenings he would take out the journal and read a page or two for comfort and guidance. The last entry was especially meaningful to him.

> Written in view of my approaching end, which has often lately seemed so near, but just now, almost imminent. I want to write while I have the power to do it.
>
> Well, glory to God, He has enabled me to make a hard fight for the Sudan, and although it may seem like a total failure and defeat, it is not. We shall have the victory. I have no regret for undertaking this venture, and in this manner my life has not been thrown away. My only regrets are for my poor dear mother. For her sake I would have chosen to live.

Rowland knew he would have to visit Mrs. Gowans as soon as he reached Canada. Although he had already written a letter informing her of Walter's death, he felt burdened at the thought of seeing her in person. However, when he finally reached Toronto, Mrs. Gowans greeted Rowland as if he were her lost son.

"You may be worried about me, Mr. Bingham," Mrs. Gowans said, clasping his hands in hers, "but you need not be. I would rather have had Walter go out to the Sudan and die there all alone than have him home today disobeying the Lord. I pray every day that God will raise up a Christian witness in Girku, where he laid down his life for the gospel."

Rowland was amazed at her determination and commitment to see the work of the Sudan Interior Mission continue, and he promised to look for ways to continue it. It was not easy, however. Although no one actually came right out and said the words, "I told you so; any man going to Africa might as well pack his clothes in a coffin," Rowland knew that many Christians thought that way.

Recalling all the diseases he had seen in Africa and how he had needed to nurse Tom when he was sick with malaria, Rowland decided to get some basic medical training. A hospital in Cleveland, Ohio, offered such training, and Rowland spent several months there.

With some medical training behind him, Rowland then enrolled in the Christian and Missionary Alliance Bible College in New York City. This was the same Bible college founded by the Reverend A. B. Simpson that Walter and Tom had attended. Rowland found some comfort in knowing that he was attending the same Bible college that his two friends had graduated from just a few years earlier. Many of the faculty members still remembered the two former students and often spoke of their sacrifice for the Sudan.

After he graduated from Bible college, Rowland was asked to consider becoming the pastor of a Baptist church in Newburgh, New York, a small town on the Hudson River. Although his heart beat for Africa, he accepted the position. One reason he accepted was that it would give him time to reinvigorate the Sudan Interior Mission and, he hoped, form a board to oversee it.

Another reason he accepted the job in Newburgh was that it was closer to Toronto, where he had started seeing a young woman named Helen Elizabeth Blair. Helen was the daughter of the man who had emptied his bank account to send Rowland to Africa, and there was something about her that Rowland found especially attractive. True, Helen was beautiful, with long, honey-blonde hair and clear blue eyes, but she also had something that Rowland was inwardly attracted to. She had a strong trust in God and an iron will.

Sensing that they would make a good team, Rowland, in January 1898, asked Helen to marry him. Helen readily accepted his proposal, and soon the couple was busy making plans for a May wedding. Since Helen was a dressmaker by trade, she began buying fabric and making a wedding dress and bridesmaid dresses.

Rowland rented an unfurnished apartment in Newburgh for the couple to live in. He hoped to furnish the place with the money he raised from speaking at a month-long series of meetings at a Bible conference in Kansas, to which he had been invited as one of the speakers.

Things did not go quite as planned, however. When he arrived in Kansas, Rowland found that the Baptist churches sponsoring the Bible conference were opposed to missionary work, especially anything to do with Africa. Some time before, the churches had sent out their own band of missionaries to Africa, where they had all perished. Now Rowland was faced with a dilemma. He could stay and try to overcome the bitterness of church members toward missions, or he could leave while he still had time to go back to Newburgh and earn enough money to buy furniture for the apartment.

Rowland decided to stay, and at the end of the month, he felt he had made some progress in softening the hearts of church members toward missions. However, they did not give him anywhere near the amount of money he had hoped to make speaking at the conference. In fact, he had to use his last dollar to pay the train fare from Kansas to Toronto and on to nearby Aberfoyle, where Helen lived.

As Rowland sat for three days and three nights in coach class on the train, two matters filled his thoughts. The first was how he was going to get enough money to take Helen back to Newburgh, and the other was how they were going to get necessary items like a bed and a table and chairs once they arrived there. The first matter was dealt with when Rowland picked up his mail in Toronto. The letters carrying wedding congratulations also contained enough money for two train fares to New York State. Now Rowland waited to see how God would provide the furniture for the apartment.

That night, while staying in the Blair home in Aberfoyle, he received a telegram from the wife of a deacon in the Baptist church in Newburgh. The deacon and his wife had spent the winter in Florida because the deacon was in poor health. The telegram informed Rowland that the man had died there the week before. The deacon's wife asked Rowland if he could look after their furniture until she could come back to Newburgh and decide what to do with it. As Helen and Rowland stood at the altar on May 24, 1898, saying their vows in front of the Reverend John Salmon, their immediate future was thus secure.

Three days after the wedding, the couple was back in Newburgh. They had had plenty of time to talk on the train south from Toronto. Rowland was delighted to find that Helen was just as enthusiastic as ever about the work in Africa. By the time they arrived in Newburgh, they had made a key decision. The work of the Sudan Interior Mission needed a strong "sending team" in North America if it was to flourish and grow. As Rowland looked around for someone to take on the enormous task of leading such a team, he realized that he was the best-suited person for the job. He knew a little of Africa and the challenges that faced missionaries there. He also had a network of friends and churches that he hoped would get behind such a mission. With some reluctance at the thought of not going back to the mission field immediately, Rowland decided to form a mission board and ask the board to elect him secretary. And since he was a Baptist minister, he hoped that the Baptist church would take up the burden and make SIM a Baptist mission.

The idea of SIM's being a Baptist mission was reinforced by one of Rowland's rich friends who lived in Toronto. He promised Rowland that he would give SIM one hundred dollars a year for the first three years on the condition that the mission accept only Baptist missionaries.

The work of the Sudan Interior Mission progressed slowly, but seven months after getting married, Rowland resigned his position as pastor at Newburgh and moved with Helen to Toronto to work full-time for the mission. It was New Year's Day 1899 when they arrived in Toronto, where a hard Canadian winter had taken hold. They found a small apartment to rent and soon were settled into their new life.

It was not an easy life. There was very little money in the SIM account, and Rowland had agreed that he would not withdraw any of it to pay for his own needs. As the secretary he would trust God to provide for him and Helen outside of whatever was donated for the mission.

In February, just a month after they had arrived in Toronto, the mission was showing great signs of hope. Two young men, James Moline and Peter Taylor, had stepped forward to be missionaries to the Sudan. This time, though, Rowland did not send them directly to Lagos. He felt it was wiser to send them first to Tripoli on the north coast of Africa for six months of study in the Hausa language. There they could make a more gradual adjustment to African food and culture. The Hausa people came from the

Sudan region around Niger, and many Hausa men passed through Tripoli on trading ventures. Rowland had heard that it was easy to engage a Hausa language teacher from among these men.

While Rowland was arranging for the two men to go to Tripoli, Helen was expecting their first baby. Grace Winifred Bingham was born on December 22, 1899, three days after Rowland's twenty-seventh birthday.

Rowland and Helen continued to pray that God would provide food and shelter for them. On one such occasion, soon after Winifred was born, Rowland spent his last penny on a bus fare to visit a girls' reform school. He had been there several times before at the request of the school's superintendent, Miss Wetherford. Although the girls were in the school as an alternative to serving time in prison, they had responded heartily to the idea of missions in the Sudan. Rowland was amazed when Miss Wetherford told him that the girls had suggested giving up their free time twice a week to sew and knit items that could be sold to raise money for SIM. The girls, who called their little band the Christian Endeavor Society, began sending small amounts, and then up to one hundred dollars at a time, to the SIM fund.

On this occasion, Rowland spoke to the girls about the two young men studying the Hausa language in Tripoli and asked that they pray for them. When the meeting was over, Miss Wetherford invited Rowland to her office for a cup of tea before he left.

As she poured the tea, Miss Wetherford told Rowland that many years before, God had stirred her heart for missions and she had offered herself to the Presbyterian Church Board for China for service there. The board had turned her down because she was too old.

"Since that time," Miss Wetherford said, "I have been living for missions. All my earnings beyond meeting my bare needs have been put into the missionary treasury. Some time ago a friend of mine died and left me one hundred dollars in her will. I put it in the bank in case I lost my job or had some other kind of emergency." She paused for a moment and sipped her tea. "This morning, while you were talking to the girls, I felt I should give you that money to keep your work as secretary going. You have a lot of expenses, and I want you to take the money to help until the work gets on its feet."

Rowland put down his cup. "My dear lady," he said, "thank you so much for the offer, but I could not possibly take your last dollar. You may soon need it more than I."

"But what else can I do with it, Mr. Bingham?" she replied. "I feel that God has earmarked it for you, so I cannot keep it for myself, can I?"

"I suppose not," Rowland agreed. The tone of Miss Wetherford's voice made it clear she was a woman used to being obeyed!

That night the check for one hundred dollars lay on the dresser in Rowland and Helen's bedroom. Even though he tried to sleep, Rowland could not keep from thinking about it. The money itself was a wonderful provision, something he really needed. However, it was not the money but the person who gave it to him that kept Rowland awake. *It doesn't seem right,* he thought, *that today a Presbyterian woman gave all the money she possessed to enable me to start a Baptist mission work in the Sudan. Yet, while I might take her last dollar, if she herself were to apply to serve in the mission she would not be accepted because she is a Presbyterian.*

Rowland wrestled with the problem all night, and by dawn he had made up his mind: SIM would be open to accept missionaries from all denominations, not just Baptists. He wondered what the Baptist church would think about this. And what about his friend who had promised him one hundred dollars a year if he kept the mission under the Baptist umbrella?

Rowland knew what he had to do. As soon as he could get away, he went to see the man who had made the offer and told him that he could no longer accept the hundred dollars because he did not believe the Sudan Interior Mission should be for the Baptists alone.

Surprisingly, as Rowland explained the situation, his friend chuckled and said, "God has challenged me on the same issue. Instead of a hundred dollars a year for the first three years, I will make it one thousand dollars a year for that period, and if you go overseas with this new work, you can count on me to personally support you."

Of course this money went into the SIM missionary fund and not directly to help the Binghams with their living expenses. Because of this, things sometimes got to the point where Rowland and Helen had little food left in the house. Only once did they find they had nothing but milk and butter. And on that occasion God provided for them through their landlord.

The landlord, Mr. McCormick, who lived next door, was also the local grocer. He allowed the Binghams to keep food in the shop's refrigerator, since they did not have one of their own. On that night Rowland watched over Winifred as she slept in her crib while Helen returned the milk and butter to the refrigerator. The milk was for the baby, and they had nothing to use the butter on.

Several minutes later Helen burst back into the apartment with a jubilant expression on her face. "Guess what?" she said. Before Rowland could say anything, she produced a loaf of rye bread from behind her back. "Mr. McCormick gave this to me. He said the baker dropped off some samples of rye bread, and he wants us to taste it and tell him what we think!" She laughed, and Rowland joined in.

"I think we are going to find it quite delicious, don't you?" Rowland eventually said.

God always seemed to provide for the Binghams. Sometimes it was at the last minute, but Rowland and Helen never sat down to an empty plate. Such provision was a comforting thought to Rowland as he thought of the months ahead. Several weeks before, James Moline and Peter Taylor had returned to Toronto in good health, having mastered the basics of the Hausa language. Now Rowland planned to accompany them to Africa to help get them established in the Sudan, where the work of SIM could begin in earnest. Since Africa was no place for a woman with a baby to care for, Helen and Winifred would stay behind.

On January 11, 1900, Rowland and the two missionaries set out for Africa. It had been a little over six years since Rowland had made the same journey with Walter Gowans and Tom Kent. Before he left, Rowland paid a visit to Mrs. Gowans, who wished him well and offered her full support for the mission, promising to pray for them every day.

After the ship reached Liverpool, England, on January 27, Rowland enjoyed a reunion with his family. His mother was still in fine health, and most of his brothers were married with children of their own. His sister, Winifred, was still single, however, and very interested in Christian missions. Rowland encouraged her to be a prayer link in SIM's chain of supporters and to consider emigrating to Canada to help with the office work there when the mission got larger.

A month later, on February 27, the group sailed from Liverpool for Lagos, a journey that took them three weeks.

As he had done on the earlier trip with Walter and Tom, Rowland found a place to rent, and he and James and Peter moved in. Once settled in the house, it did not take Rowland long to realize that the missionaries in Lagos were even more opposed to their planned mission than they had been the previous time. They tried to discourage James and Peter with stories of the hardships they would encounter if they ventured into the interior, not to mention the number and circumstances of those missionaries who had died in the process. Rowland did his best to encourage the young men as he made plans to journey inland with them. But three weeks after he arrived in Lagos, Rowland once again came down with malaria. As his condition deteriorated, the other two men took him to the hospital, where a doctor ordered that he return home as quickly as possible. Rowland was too sick to argue, and so he was carried on a stretcher and put aboard a ship bound for England.

As they left him feverish and sweating on his bunk, James and Peter promised Rowland that they would stay in Africa and carry on the work of SIM. Rowland was confident they would. After all, they had already spent six months in Tripoli learning the Hausa language and acclimatizing to conditions in Africa.

As the ship sailed away from Lagos, Rowland felt defeated. In fact, he had never felt so low in all his life. Yet he clung to the hope that James and Peter would succeed in their mission. They were better equipped for Africa than he or Walter and Tom had been.

By the time the ship reached Plymouth, England, on April 27, 1900, Rowland was feeling much better.

The attention of the doctor on board, plus the cool sea breeze, had worked wonders. Rowland looked forward to news from Lagos as he made his way to London to pick up his mail. He found a telegram waiting for him. The words on it turned his blood cold: "Following you home. Work impossible. Need advice and rest. Moline and Taylor."

For a brief moment Rowland wondered whether it would have been easier to die in Africa than to live to read this message. He could hardly bear to think about the opportunity these two young men had missed and the setback this would be to the credibility of SIM. So far the mission had not managed to keep a single missionary on the field.

With a heavy heart Rowland booked passage for Canada. He dreaded meeting with the board of the Sudan Interior Mission in Toronto. What if they decided to give up? What would he do then?

Chapter 8

One Step Forward and Two Steps Back

Finally the moment Rowland Bingham dreaded arrived. He was standing before the board of SIM in Toronto, explaining why the latest missionary attempt had ended in complete failure. None of the men on the board said anything unkind, but they did not say anything encouraging either—except for one man, Bill Henderson.

After the meeting ended, Bill sought to encourage Rowland. "Don't give up," he said. "God will give you a breakthrough if you stay true to your calling."

Rowland took Bill's words to heart and determined to go on. He continued to speak in churches and public meetings, raising awareness and funds for the Sudan Interior Mission. In the meantime the Bingham family managed to live on ten dollars a month, hardly enough to pay the rent, but somehow enough to get by. When a second daughter, Marianne, arrived, Rowland felt the weight of responsibility for his growing family.

Rowland marveled at Helen's ability to make the best out of whatever was at hand. Helen sewed all their clothes and turned the collars on Rowland's shirts so that they would last twice as long. She also made Winifred pretty clothes cut from the fabric of old garments and made diapers for Marianne out of old flannel sheets. The Binghams were determined to do whatever was needed to make SIM successful.

Amazingly, by the end of 1901, four more men had stepped forward to go as SIM missionaries to Africa: Edward Anthony, Alex Banfield, Charles Robinson, and Albert Taylor (who was no relation to Peter Taylor, who had gone out before). This time Rowland decided not to go with them to Africa. There was a lot of work to be done in Canada if more young men were to be sent out to the Sudan. Rowland also feared that if he went, the men might come to rely too much on him as their leader, and if he were struck down with malaria again, they might not know how to go on without him.

In February 1902 two of the men, Edward and Charles, were sent off to Tripoli to learn the Hausa language. Alex and Albert, both of whom had had little formal schooling, were sent on a tour of the Zambesi Industrial Mission, located on the eastern coast of Africa. They were instructed to study the way this group helped train Africans for technical jobs, in the hope that similar methods could be used in the Sudan.

After six months of learning, the four men reunited in England before setting out for the Sudan. They were all still healthy and ready to serve.

During the time the men were away training, the British had sent troops to break the power of the slave-trading Muslim kings in the Sudan. The expedition, which was led by Sir Fredrick Lugard, was successful, and in 1903 Nigeria, located on the western edge of the Sudan, became a British protectorate and part of the British Empire.

While in Britain, Alex wrote to Rowland to say that he had met with Sir Fredrick Lugard, who was home arranging the new administration for Nigeria. Sir Fredrick told Alex that it was the official policy of the government that the Muslim states of northern Nigeria were forbidden territory to Christian missionaries, but he would do whatever he could to help missionaries enter southern Nigeria. He even suggested that the four missionaries sail back to Africa on the same ship with him so that he could assist them in traveling up the Niger River upon their arrival and help them settle inland.

All of this was wonderful news to Rowland. Finally something seemed to be turning out right! Rowland waited eagerly for the next installment of news from the men. He was thankful that these men were sturdier than the previous missionaries had been.

The men soon reported that they had all made it five hundred miles up the Niger River to a village named Patigi. They had set up camp three miles up a track on the western bank of the river. Rowland had advised them to camp away from the edge of the river, because he had observed that the edges of the rivers always seemed to be the most unhealthy places in Africa.

The four young missionaries proved to be practical. Alex sent back sketches to Rowland of the headquarters they were constructing from bricks they made themselves. When the building was finished, Rowland received a photograph of it. It was a large, oval shape with a low mud brick wall and high pitched grass roof.

The news that SIM missionaries finally had a toehold in the Sudan created more interest from people about the mission. One day, soon after Rowland received the photograph from Patigi, a man knocked at the door of the Binghams' apartment and introduced himself.

"My name is Andrew Stirrett," the man said, holding up a copy of *A Plea for the Central Sudan,* a tract Rowland had penned several months before. "Are you the Reverend Bingham, the man who wrote this tract?"

"Yes," Rowland said, surveying the short man in front of him. "That's me. Would you like to come in, Mr. Stirrett?"

Soon Andrew was seated in the living room drinking coffee and telling his story. "I am a pharmacist," he began, "and I have had some small success in the business. As well, I have just completed the requirements for a medical degree to become a doctor. I now plan to go to England to take a special tropical medicine course. Anyway, the point is, I went back to get my degree because I felt the call to be a missionary somewhere. I didn't quite know where until I read this tract." He held up *A Plea for the Central Sudan* once again. "It so moved my heart that I have not been able to think of anything else. I am desperate to get there. Could you use me?"

Rowland did not need to think about his answer! A man with medical knowledge would be a tremendous asset to the mission. Just as he was about to answer the question, Andrew interrupted his thoughts.

"I need you to tell me honestly," he continued, boring into Rowland with his intense brown eyes. "If you do not think I am the man to go, I want to sell all of my property and give the money to someone else who is going."

Rowland was impressed with the earnestness of this man and felt sure that Andrew had the makings of a good missionary.

As the two men continued talking, Rowland encouraged Andrew to go to England for the tropical medicine course. He also gave him an SIM application form to fill out. A week later Andrew returned the form, which greatly pleased Rowland, until he read the date 1865. That was Andrew Stirrett's birth year, which meant that Andrew was thirty-seven years old! Rowland would never have guessed he was that old. Andrew had looked to Rowland to be not a day over twenty-five. A person of thirty-seven was considered by the SIM board to be too old for missionary service. He could hardly be expected to survive in such an extreme environment as Africa. But what was Rowland to say to this enthusiastic pharmacist who was willing to give all he had for the Sudan? Rather than turning him down flat, the board decided to investigate how other mission organizations handled older applicants.

While the board was doing this, Rowland received a letter from Andrew saying that he had sold his drug business and was leaving all his property, which included two stores with four apartments above them, plus thousands of dollars worth of stocks and bonds, to the mission. Andrew also said he was working his way to England by caring for cattle aboard a cattle boat to attend the tropical medicine course.

Rowland was flabbergasted. This was a huge sum of money. He felt there was no way he could accept it, especially since everything had happened so quickly. Together with the board, he decided to put everything that belonged to Andrew Stirrett into a trust fund so that it would not be touched for at least four years, when Andrew would have had ample time to reconsider his generous gift and take it back if he wanted to.

Three months later, Andrew wrote again to say that he had finished his course in tropical medicine and could not wait any longer for an answer from SIM. He was on his way to Africa and would be grateful if Rowland could write straight to the SIM missionaries at Patigi and tell them whether or not he had been accepted into the mission. If the answer was no, he would simply find a way to share the gospel with the local people himself. Rowland wrote to Patigi, suggesting that the SIM missionaries there receive Andrew and see how he coped with the climate and conditions.

In the meantime, news of Sir Fredrick Lugard's British troops gave everyone cause for concern. Sir Fredrick had set up his headquarters in Jebba, right on the Niger River. Now, one year later, nearly 90 percent of his men either were dead and buried or had been transported back to England seriously ill. Only ten soldiers from every hundred that came to Africa were still standing, and some of them just barely.

This horrific death toll among the British army had one unexpected positive result for missionaries. Since malaria had killed most of the soldiers, a prominent tropical disease expert named Dr. Donald Ross was sent out to investigate. For five or six years, evidence had been growing that malaria was a disease that occurred around swamps and rivers because these bodies of water harbored mosquitoes and that it was actually these mosquitoes that carried the disease and infected humans. Dr. Ross's visit to Nigeria confirmed this to the British government, which established guidelines for avoiding the deadly disease.

Now that it was known that mosquitoes were the carriers of malaria, the missionaries began using nets to sleep under at night, wore cool, long-sleeved clothing, and used various oils and potions to repel the insects. With these precautions and the use of quinine to treat the disease early, the rate of malaria cases began to drop. Sadly, it was not in time for Charles Robinson and Edward Anthony, both of whom lasted less than two years in Africa before returning home because of illness.

By the end of 1903, however, eight more missionaries had signed up with SIM to go to Africa, though five of them resigned and returned home soon after arriving and experiencing the conditions at Patigi, and one of them died there of blackwater fever.

It seemed to Rowland that the mission was taking one step forward and two steps back a lot of the time, but he refused to give up. And Helen stood staunchly behind him. They both believed that with God's help the Sudan Interior Mission would one day be a strong missionary force in Africa.

As 1904 rolled around, something unexpected helped Rowland to keep the dream of SIM alive: a Christian newspaper. *The Faithful Witness* was the only Christian newspaper in Canada that was interdenominational. The editor, Bill Henderson, a member of SIM's board, sometimes asked Rowland to write a missionary section for the paper. In 1904 Bill paid a visit to Rowland. He looked nervous from the start and took little time in getting to the point. "Reverend Bingham, as you know, *The Faithful Witness* has been losing money for the past several years."

Rowland nodded. He was aware that the newspaper was not a profitable enterprise, but he believed it was a vital one.

"I have managed to put enough of my own money into it to keep it running," Bill continued, fidgeting with the rim of his felt hat. "However, I have run up against hard times and can no longer afford to do that. To put it plainly, I am going to have to discontinue publication."

"I'm sorry to hear that," Rowland replied. "Is there anything I can do to help?"

"I have been thinking about what could be done, and your name keeps coming to mind. I was wondering if you would like to take over the paper and give it more of a missionary emphasis. It won't cost you anything, not to buy it at least, though I can't say how you would have any more chance of making enough to keep it afloat than I did. Still, what do you say? Is it of interest to you?"

Rowland's mind whirled with ideas. There were so many good missionary stories to be told, so many prayer needs to be presented, and he could see the possibilities right away.

He told Bill that he would pray about it. A week later he was certain that God wanted him to take over the failing publication. The SIM board promised to give the new venture support in any way it could other than financially, so Rowland waited for events to unfold.

It did not take long. Rowland received a letter from a woman in New England who had read that

The Faithful Witness was ceasing publication. The woman urged Rowland to find another way to get the missionary message out. Rowland replied to her letter that he had in fact been offered the newspaper but did not have the resources at present to carry it on. Within two weeks he received another letter from the woman, along with a check to cover the first year's printing and mailing costs!

And so Rowland found himself launched into Christian journalism. He changed the name of the paper to *The Evangelical Christian* and opened it up so that any Christian mission or organization could use it as a voice to the Christians of Canada. Some on the board of SIM were not happy about this. They felt that Rowland should concentrate most of the articles in the paper on what was happening within the Sudan Interior Mission. However, Rowland refused to narrow down the focus of *The Evangelical Christian* that much. He told those who grumbled that God was big enough to call people to give and pray and go to all the various missions that were reported on in the paper.

The newspaper kept Rowland very busy, and he soon enlisted Helen to do a lot of the writing and supervision of the printing. With Helen working on this important voice for Christian missions, Rowland was free to turn his attention to SIM and its missionaries. God had given the pioneer mission a toehold in the Sudan, and Rowland knew that only God could lead them on the path that lay ahead.

Chapter 9

The Turning of the Tide

The years rolled by and the work of the Sudan Interior Mission began to grow. Andrew Stirrett proved to be well suited to life in Africa. He was a tireless worker whose stamina amazed the younger missionaries. And two new missionaries were now serving with the mission in Nigeria. The first was Tommie Titcombe, a short man with little formal education. When Rowland had asked him what he would do if SIM turned him down, he replied, "I'll find a board to send me, even if it is a washboard!"

Eventually, in 1908, the board of SIM did send out Tommie Titcombe, who went straight to work among the Yagba people in the town of Egbe. The other man SIM sent out was a well-known Canadian athlete named Guy Playfair. Guy had attended

Moody Bible Institute in Chicago and then left straightaway for the Sudan.

In addition, an SIM office had been started in England to recruit and support missionaries from that country.

Winifred, Rowland's only sister, came to Canada to visit him and stayed on to help him and Helen with their ever-increasing workload. She arrived just in time to help Rowland launch his latest project—a new Christian publishing house called Evangelical Publishers. The idea was the result of the many letters Rowland had received as the editor of *The Evangelical Christian.* In the seven years he had been overseeing the paper, letters had poured in from Canada and abroad asking his advice and guidance on where to find good Christian books or how to get one published. After a lot of prayer and heart searching, Rowland gathered a group of ten Christian men, formed a board, and set up the publishing house.

The first thing the board came up with was a simple charter that expressed everything Rowland believed.

> Our Purpose: To preach the gospel and build up believers in the Faith. To defend the Faith against heresies and inspire missionary activity everywhere.
>
> Our Platform: Salvation by Christ
> Separation unto Christ
> Working with Christ
> Waiting for Christ

> Our Guarantee: We will never knowingly handle any literature which is not in accord with the fundamentals of the Word of God, as set forth in our Doctrinal statement.

The board also decided that any profits made from the sale of the books published would be plowed back into printing free books and tracts to distribute to those who did not know Christ. Once again, Rowland had set up a ministry that was aimed at drawing Christians together and inspiring them to go to the mission field. The offices for the new publishing house were squeezed into *The Evangelical Christian* headquarters on College Street in Toronto.

Rowland never allowed other projects to cloud his commitment to "his" missionaries. He constantly looked for ways to support and encourage them. Numerous letters went back and forth between Toronto and the Sudan offering advice and counsel.

But there was nothing like actually being in the field and seeing things firsthand. So, late in 1913, Rowland decided that the following year he would travel to Nigeria with six new missionary appointees and see for himself all the new mission stations that were popping up.

In the summer of 1914, Dr. Herbert MacKenzie, founder of the Erieside Bible Conference, invited Rowland to speak at the conference. As Rowland spoke about the work in the Sudan, Dr. MacKenzie became very interested in SIM and asked if he could accompany Rowland to Africa to see the work for himself. Everything was arranged, and on August 3, Rowland was thinking how smoothly things were going when he picked up the evening newspaper. The headline that greeted him read, "ultimatum to germany—war with britain within twenty-four hours unless germany ceases to advance into belgium."

Rowland's first thought was for the missionaries in the field. If Britain went to war, it would undoubtedly cut off the flow of money in and out of the country. Rowland sent an urgent telegram to SIM's British office instructing it to send all the money it had on hand, including that in trust funds, to Nigeria. This was done just in the nick of time; the following day the newspaper headlines screamed three words: "britain declares war."

Most of Rowland's friends tried to dissuade him and Herbert MacKenzie from going ahead with their plan to visit Africa. Heading out of the country when Germany was advancing seemed like an unwise plan. What if the ship they were to travel on was torpedoed at sea, or what if they could not get back to Canada?

Rowland and Herbert prayed about the situation and decided to go ahead with their plan. If ever missionaries needed encouragement, it was when they were cut off from their homeland by war.

In Toronto Rowland began making final preparations for the trip. Yet, even on an official trip like this, he refused to allow SIM funds to be used to pay his passage to and from Africa. Instead he prayed that God would provide the money needed for his passage. That way he felt that he was not taking anything away from the missionaries in the field.

When the trip was only three days away, Rowland was still waiting to see how God would provide the money for his fare. The money came the following day in the form of a check for one hundred dollars. An old friend had sent it to him along with a letter explaining that several of his children had been ill with diphtheria and God had spared all their lives. As a gesture of thanks to God, the man had sent off a check to Rowland. It was enough money for Rowland to get across the Atlantic Ocean to England, where he trusted that God would provide the rest of the money he needed.

Ships crossing the Atlantic Ocean at this time were in special danger. The Germans picked them off with torpedoes fired from their long-range U-boats. When the ship Rowland, Herbert, and the six new missionaries were traveling on was midway across the Atlantic, the captain announced a change of plans. The vessel would be docking in Glasgow, Scotland, and not Liverpool, England, as planned. That way it would sail up the west coast of Ireland before looping east for Glasgow and not follow the planned route around the south of Ireland and up through the Irish Sea to Liverpool. The change was made because the Canadian ship ahead of them had been torpedoed and sunk by the Germans, and so they were taking evasive action.

When the ship finally arrived in Glasgow, Rowland discovered that word of the group's coming had somehow reached the local churches, and a hearty welcome awaited the travelers. Since he was in Glasgow, Rowland was able to meet up with an old friend, Pastor Findlay. As a gesture of support for the work of SIM, Pastor Findlay and his congregation paid to outfit the entire party of missionaries for Africa. Pastor Findlay also went on to quiz Rowland about his own finances.

"How are you fixed personally for the journey you are going on?" he asked Rowland as they sat eating dinner together the night before they were all to set sail for Africa.

Rowland gave him the answer he always gave to people who asked such questions. "Pastor Findlay, when I go on the Master's business, He generally looks after the fixing for me."

The pastor would not let Rowland off the hook so easily. "That is not an answer to my question. Do you have money for the journey?" he asked directly.

Now Rowland felt that he had to tell him the truth. "I have provisions for all of my party but not for myself," he said, watching as a smile spread over Pastor Findlay's face.

"You stay here and chat with Mrs. Findlay. I am going up to my room for a moment. I am going to have a hand in this pie!" the pastor said as he scooted away from the table.

Pastor Findlay returned several minutes later and presented Rowland with a check. "Half of this will cover your expenses," he said, "and the other half is for you to give away as you choose. Out on the field you will see missionaries who could use five or ten pounds to encourage them along."

Rowland hardly knew how to say thank you for such a large gift, especially after all Pastor Findlay and his church had already done for the party of missionaries accompanying him.

The next day they set sail for Africa. As Rowland stood on the deck watching the docks of Glasgow disappear from view, he could not help but think of his last time in Africa. Fourteen years had passed since he had been carried, desperately ill, aboard a ship returning to England, only to have the two missionaries he had left behind to establish the work of SIM follow him home three weeks later. How impossible everything had seemed back then. Now there were ten SIM workers in the field and another six aboard ship with him and Herbert MacKenzie.

As the ship made its way down the west coast of Africa, Rowland's excitement grew. He could hardly wait to see the SIM missionaries and the work they were doing.

They dropped anchor off Lagos in early December, twenty-one years to the day since Rowland, Walter Gowans, and Tom Kent had arrived there. It seemed like nothing had changed in Lagos. The same crowd of men were lined along the dock waiting for their lighter to dock. The same cooking odors filled the air, as did the ubiquitous dust. Rowland relished it all as he stepped onto African soil once again.

After clearing customs, Rowland began making plans for the six missionaries who had arrived with him to travel inland to Minna, where they were to study language for their first year in Africa. Once they had left for Minna, Rowland was delighted to learn that the first scheduled event he was to attend was a missionary conference Tommie Titcombe had organized at Egbe. Tommie had prepared everything and soon arrived in Lagos to escort Rowland and Herbert to Egbe.

As they walked the bush paths into the interior, Tommie told the amazing story of how the Yagba tribe had opened up to the gospel. Rowland had read about this in letters Tommie had sent to him in Toronto, but it was much more thrilling to hear Tommie tell the story in person.

Just seven years before, there had been only one Christian in Egbe. His name was Dani, and as a small child, he had been captured by a slave raider and taken from Egbe to the coast. There he eventually was freed and started attending a Baptist church. He learned to read and bought a Yoruba Bible, which he could read because it was written in a dialect similar to Yagba, which Dani spoke. As a result, Dani became a Christian.

Finally, when he was in his thirties, Dani felt compelled to return to Egbe. Back in Egbe, he began reading his Bible aloud in the marketplace and was able to interest four young men in the gospel. Together Dani and the four young men walked to the lone mission station at Patigi to ask for their own missionary. As soon as Tommie arrived in Africa, he was sent to the Yagba tribe, even though he had no language training and had no clue how to speak their strange language. But Tommie persevered, and now there were over a thousand Christian converts in the tribe.

Rowland, Herbert, and Tommie arrived in Egbe on New Year's Day 1915. And what a day it was for Rowland. As they neared the town, the last few miles led up a green slope past several hills that bordered Egbe. As they walked, a group of young boys came running out to meet them. Men and women, dressed in their best clothes, also came to greet them. Then, at the top of the slope, King Agbana of Egbe was carried in his hammock to welcome them. He greeted Rowland graciously and offered him his hammock. Rowland turned down the offer, preferring to walk with the procession of people that surged around them.

By the time they had reached the mission station on the edge of Egbe, tears were streaming down Rowland's face. Rowland was not a man to get overly emotional, but the sight of so many joyful Africans touched him deeply. All the effort and sacrifice that had gone into establishing the Sudan Interior Mission seemed worth it. That night, as the Christians of the town gathered to hear Rowland speak, he told them how he wished all the people who had given to and prayed for the work of SIM could see their happy faces.

Andrew Stirrett had also come to the conference, and Rowland had a delightful reunion with him. For Rowland, though, the highlight of the conference came at the end, when he, Andrew, and Herbert had the privilege of baptizing 111 new believers. That alone made worthwhile all the heartaches that Rowland had endured over the years establishing SIM.

In Egbe, Rowland also got to meet Dani and the original band of young men who had asked for a missionary to come to their tribe. Rowland had prayed often for them over the years, and now he was able to shake their hands in person and greet them warmly.

Rowland wished that Helen and all the SIM supporters could have been there with him to see the astounding sight, a sight that the missionaries in Lagos had declared would never happen. He was buoyed with the hope that the tide was turning for missions in Africa.

The day after the baptism service, Rowland looked out the door of the mission station to see about one hundred women waiting for him. He stepped outside and called Tommie to translate for him so that he could find out what the women wanted.

It soon became clear enough. "The missionary has taught us a lot, but he is a man," they said. "Have you no white sister in your country who will come out and be a missionary to us women? If we had a white sister, there are so many things we could ask her that we want to know."

Rowland was surprised by their request, though as he talked it over with Tommie, he came to understand some of the reasons why they wanted a woman missionary. One of the most pressing needs was health education. About 85 percent of their babies died within a year of birth, a grim statistic in any country. Many of the deaths were caused by the belief that breast milk was rotten until the ninth day after the baby was born. Because of this belief, new mothers would not feed their babies breast milk, choosing instead to give them filthy rags soaked in river water to suck on. The resulting infections killed thousands of babies each year.

The Christian women of the Yagba tribe knew there must be a better way to keep their babies alive. They just needed another woman to show them how. They also needed a woman missionary to shelter them in case they had twins. Their witch doctors told them that all twins were the children of evil spirits and had to be killed at birth. Often the mother was killed along with the twins. And although there were now many Christians in the town, no one had ever managed to keep newborn twins from being killed. Not one pair had survived.

Rowland was touched by the women's request and relieved to know that a solution was in sight. Tommie's fiancée, Ethel McIntosh, was one of the missionaries who had arrived with him. She was now in Minna undertaking language study, and she and Tommie would be married at the end of the year, when her language training would be over.

Greatly pleased by what he had seen in Egbe, Rowland took numerous notes so that he could give a full report when he returned to Canada.

It was not just existing mission stations that Rowland had in mind to visit. Northern Nigeria still had vast regions that were under Muslim domination and totally closed to the gospel. One exception was the village of Girku, where three Church Missionary Society missionaries had set up a small station. When Rowland heard about it, he decided to visit it.

Girku was the same village where Walter Gowans had died, and in fact, his death had led to the opening of a mission station there. Rowland learned that a leader in the Church of England named Bishop Tugwell had heard of Walter's and Tom's deaths, as well as the deaths of Bishop Hill and the others who had tried to get into the Sudan interior. Touched by their dedication, Bishop Tugwell rallied five missionaries to make another attempt at penetrating the interior. Unlike those before them, this group made it all the way to Kano. However, as soon as the Muslim emir, who was a slave-raiding ruler, learned of their purpose, he gave them three days to leave the city. The six men fled to the next city, Zaria, where they received the same response.

From Zaria the six headed out into the desert, not knowing where to go next. It was then that they stumbled upon the village of Girku, where they found people unlike any others they had met in the interior. These people welcomed the missionaries into their village and gave them a hut to live in. The missionaries stayed there for two years preaching the gospel and helping the people. Although there were few converts, the people remained open to missionaries.

Rowland, accompanied by Herbert and Andrew, set out on the long trek to visit Walter Gowans's grave. When they reached Girku, Andrew had no difficulty in locating the hut where Walter had died. The same couple who had offered shelter to Walter still lived in the hut.

The hut itself was a small structure about eight feet square and made of mudded walls with a woven grass roof. It stood at the corner of a cornfield, and when the old woman saw the three men coming, she called her husband in from hoeing weeds with a sharpened stick. Using Andrew as his interpreter, Rowland explained that he was a friend of the white man who had died in their hut many years before.

The old woman nodded. "I remember it well," she replied.

"Do you have children?" Rowland asked her through Andrew.

Once again the woman nodded and gestured to the right, where a group of huts stood together.

"Then," Rowland continued, "I think you would like to know that the man who died in your hut had a mother. Her name was Mrs. Gowans, and she was happy for her son to come all the way to Africa on a boat and risk sickness and death because he wanted to tell you about the great God who loves us all. The one true God had a son, and He named Him Jesus. The man who died here came to tell you about Jesus, and ever since his mother found out he died here, she has been praying for you and the other members of the village, that you would come to know that Jesus."

Rowland stopped talking. He watched as the old woman took off her only piece of jewelry, a simple gold ring. The woman held the ring out to him. "Here, take this back to the mother, and thank her that she blesses us and does not curse us."

Next the old couple showed the men where Walter's grave was. Rowland placed a cross on top of it, and the three men said a prayer together. Rowland felt much better now that he could tell Mrs. Gowans he had visited the place where Walter laid down his life.

At the grave Rowland made a silent pledge to do whatever he could to open these areas up to the gospel, even if it meant risking his life to do so.

Chapter 10

Into Tangale Territory

Rowland and Herbert spent six months visiting all eight Sudan Interior Mission stations. They covered hundreds of miles on foot or on bicycles under the harsh African sun. Still, Rowland was glad to be able to see all that was going on. He not only offered suggestions and advice but he also observed what worked, then took those ideas from one mission station to the next.

In June Herbert had to return to his church in Canada. After Herbert's departure, Rowland planned a trip to a tribe who had no Christian witness among them. These people were called the Tangale, and they lived 250 miles to the northeast of Miango, SIM's farthest outpost. It would take at least two weeks to cover that distance on foot—that is, if anyone dared walk in a straight line to get there. It was not an adventure for the fainthearted. To get there, one would have to pass through territory of ten other tribes, some of whom were known to be cannibals, while others killed men with peeled skin (white men) on sight. However, Rowland felt a strong urge to reach the Tangale people. He invited Andrew and another missionary, Norman Davis, to accompany him.

The trip started routinely enough, with ten to twelve hours of walking a day. After about seven days, they reached a group of light-skinned nomadic cattle herders called the Fulani people. Andrew had learned their language so that he could preach to them in the marketplace when their trading enterprises brought them down to Patigi. The Fulani had made a simple and temporary village out of cornstalks, and they invited the three men to stay the night with them. It turned out to be a longer stay, however, because Norman came down with a bad case of dysentery. He became so weak that Andrew came to Rowland with the worst possible news: he believed that Norman was too ill to survive.

Together Rowland and Andrew decided they should share the news with Norman, in case he had any last words he wanted written down. When Rowland told him he would probably be dying within a few hours, Norman smiled and said, "I thought I was coming out to live for the Lord, but if He wants me to die, He knows His own business best."

Once again Rowland was humbled by the attitude of an SIM missionary, and he knew he would never forget Norman's reply. Alas, soon he had more to be concerned about. Andrew also came down with dysentery, leaving Rowland to nurse them both. Rowland knew how to look after a patient with dysentery, but the two men needed one thing they had run out of—clean water. They had carried some with them, but by now it was all gone. The only water source in the village was a large, circular hollow that filled up in the rainy season. Now, toward the end of the dry season, the water was muddy, and every person, horse, cow, and pig in the village drank from it.

Rowland knew that without fresh water the two men were likely to die and that he was in great danger of getting sick himself if he drank the village water. He thus decided to try to move the two sick men to a campsite near a riverbank five miles away.

Rowland arranged for Norman and Andrew, who were both drifting in and out of consciousness, to be carried shoulder-high on their camp beds to the new location. It was quite a struggle to convince the Africans to help him carry the two men that far, but eventually Rowland managed to get everything relocated to the riverbank. He then sent a runner back to the nearest SIM station for help.

Although the water in the river was a muddy brown color, it was running fast, and Rowland decided it would be a lot safer than the water in the village. By the time help arrived two weeks later,

Andrew and Norman both appeared to be on a slow road to recovery.

When Rowland broke the news to the two men that he was sending them back to the mission station at Miango and going on alone, Andrew was indignant. "No!" he said. "If you can get me a horse, I can sit in the saddle and go on to the Tangale with you."

Rowland did not want to strain Andrew anymore, but Andrew was so insistent that Rowland eventually relented, and the two of them journeyed on together. They had one horse between them and several African porters to carry their camping equipment. However, it was hard to keep the porters moving forward, especially once they entered Tangale territory. The Tangale people often killed their enemies and used a stone to mark the place where they had buried the skulls of their victims. As the men neared Kaltungo, the first of two Tangale towns, they saw more and more marker stones placed along the roadside.

Rowland and Andrew stopped to pray before they entered Kaltungo, but when they entered the town, they were greeted with apathy. Andrew spoke fluent Hausa, which some of the Tangale understood, but no one seemed interested in listening to the message the missionaries had brought with them. Still, during their week-long visit, the men prayed every day, asking God to send permanent missionaries to the Tangale people and to help them understand the gospel.

By mid-August it was time to head south again. The two missionaries were grateful that they were alive and that many seeds had been sown in the tribe. They were especially grateful when they left Tangale territory and were met by a horseman bearing an official letter from the British Resident of the area. The letter read:

> Dear Sirs,
>
> I understand that you are contemplating a visit to the Tangale tribe. On no account are you to undertake this journey. They are currently at war, and I do not have soldiers to send with you to protect you among these savage people. Without soldiers you will not be safe.

"I am so sorry I did not deliver it sooner," the messenger said as he climbed off his horse. "The problem was that my horse was sick and I had to wait for it to get well again. However, the message is true. You must not go to the Tangale; they will kill you."

Rowland looked at Andrew, and he knew they were both thinking the same thing. It was God who had protected them from harm and allowed them to talk openly about Christianity to the Tangale.

The two men set up camp, and Rowland wrote a note back to the British Resident explaining that they had already been into Tangale territory. He pointed out that since they were not hurt, perhaps the time was right for missionaries to be sent in to work among these people.

On their way back to Patigi, the two men picked up Norman, who was now feeling much better, at Miango.

When they finally reached the mission station at Patigi, Rowland was eager to hear news of home. The Great War had seemed so far away when he was hiking through the bush, but as the other missionaries showed him newspaper clippings from Europe, the grim reality settled on him again. He read how the Germans had sunk a huge passenger liner named the *Lusitania.* Rowland recalled once seeing the vessel tied up in Liverpool, and he could easily believe the reports that over one thousand people had died when the ship was torpedoed off the south coast of Ireland as it made its way from New York to Liverpool. The newspaper clippings reported that Americans were aboard and that President Wilson was so incensed by the German aggression that he was considering committing the United States to the war.

It was not until Rowland settled down to read his own mail that he learned the sad news that his sister, Winifred, had been aboard the *Lusitania* and had perished when the ship was torpedoed. Helen wrote that Winifred had decided to return to England to fetch their mother and bring her to Canada.

At that moment Rowland wished he could be at home comforting his mother and wife, but it was not possible. Instead he wrote letters home. And in an open letter to be published in *The Evangelical Christian,* he wrote:

> Merely to mark time in missionary work during the war is a fatal blunder. We must go forward. Let the call of Christ be heard and heeded through the din of the world's conflict, and let the Church rise to a worthy endeavor to accomplish speedily the work entrusted to her.

Late in 1915 Rowland said farewell to Africa once again. He had walked over fifteen hundred miles through the interior, visiting every SIM worker and mission station and gaining a great deal of information to take home with him.

When he arrived home in Toronto, Rowland found that Helen had handled all her responsibilities remarkably well. She had a knack for editing the newspaper, and the two girls were thriving. By now Rowland's mother had come from England to stay with them, and Helen's mother was living with them too, making quite a houseful.

On top of this houseful of people, every missionary who went out to the field stayed in the Bingham house before he or she left. This was so that Rowland and Helen could get to know the missionaries and assess where they might best fit in the mission. In addition to this, many missionaries passed through and stayed in the Binghams' home on furlough.

Soon more sad news arrived at the Bingham house. Two of Rowland's younger brothers had been killed in the fighting—William in France and Harold off the coast of Tangier. But the work of SIM did not stop because of the war. By the time the conflict ended in 1918, a party of nine more missionaries had been sent out, bringing the total number of SIM missionaries now in Africa to forty-five.

This new batch of missionaries included two bright young men, John Hall and Gordon Beacham. They were both from the Reverend Herbert MacKenzie's church, where Rowland had first met them at the church's Annual Missionary Day. That day he had described the visit to the Tangale tribe and explained how much the Tangale needed their own missionaries. When they heard this, the two young men volunteered to set out for Africa almost immediately.

In the midst of all these goings-on, Rowland's mother died. At her funeral Rowland recalled the way her heart had softened toward missions over the years. He was glad that she had lived long enough to see the Sudan Interior Mission firmly established on African soil.

There was another family event around this time too, a happier event. While Rowland had been away, his daughter Winifred had been dating the young assistant editor of *The Evangelical Christian*. In 1919, Winifred Bingham and Herbert Stock were married in Toronto.

Soon after the wedding, another couple stepped forward and offered themselves for service with SIM. They were Mr. and Mrs. Ernest Jones. Although Ernest proved to be too sickly to go to Africa himself, he and his wife offered to do whatever they could to help the mission from their home in Canada. Ernest was appointed Financial and General Secretary of the mission. Creation of this new position took a lot of the stress off Rowland, freeing him to take on new projects.

One project he had been thinking about since his trip to Africa was a boarding school for the children of missionaries. When SIM began, it sent out only single, male missionaries. But single men tended to want to get married, and now there were many married couples in Africa. And as they had children, the problem of what to do with them became quite a concern. The children's health was so much more at risk in Africa than it was in Canada. Many of the missionaries in the field asked Rowland to set up a place back home where their children could come and live and study.

After praying about it, Rowland and Helen decided that this was a good idea. In 1923 they found a lovely, big home in Collingwood, Ontario, located on the shore of Georgian Bay, on Lake Huron. Rowland named it the "Gowans' Home for Missionaries' Children," and he opened it up to the children of missionaries from other mission organizations as well. Another Canadian couple took on the responsibility of being houseparents, and within a year twenty happy and healthy children were living there.

With the Gowans' Home up and running smoothly, Rowland turned to the next situation facing SIM. During the years following the Great War, Rowland had several inquiries from Australian and New Zealand Christians wanting to know how they could become involved in SIM. Since these countries were a long way from Canada, Rowland decided to go to the South Pacific himself and set up SIM offices there so that potential candidates for the mission field could be evaluated right in their home country.

When Rowland went to book passage for the trip, he found it was cheaper to buy a round-the-world ticket than to come back the same way he planned to go. So he decided to make it a trip around the world.

Not long after he had made the decision to go on the trip, Rowland was speaking at a missionary conference in Canada. At one of the meetings was a man who served on the board of a mission society that sent missionaries to India. He approached Rowland and said, "You are going to Australia. Why don't you stop off in India? If you will agree to speak to our missionaries there and stay for a month, I will pay all your stopover expenses. I would need to know your answer soon, though, so that I can arrange for all the missionaries to get together in Calcutta to hear you speak."

Rowland promised to pray about the offer that night, and the following morning he was sure that he was supposed to stop over in India, even though he had no money yet to pay for the fare he had booked.

Several days later he was explaining to two friends that he was going to deliver a series of lectures titled "Fulfilled Prophecy in the Bible" while he was in Australia. The two men asked Rowland if he would like to visit Palestine and Egypt so that he could take photographs to go with his lectures. They offered to pay his expenses to visit there on his way to Australia if he chose to do so. Once again Rowland prayed and felt that he was to make the stop in Palestine and Egypt. There was nothing he would enjoy more than to see the places where Jesus had walked and apostles had preached.

As the date for his departure drew near, Rowland had the promise of his expenses paid for a month in India and a stopover in Palestine and Egypt. Then, a week before setting sail, the staff from SIM and Evangelical Publishers presented Rowland with an envelope containing one hundred dollars. It was enough money to pay for his passage across the Atlantic Ocean to England, but no more. As he climbed aboard the *Leviathan* for the trip, Rowland wondered just how God would provide the money for the rest of his trip and what adventures he would have before he saw the shores of North America again.

Chapter 11

Around the World

Rowland found his berth on board the *Leviathan*. The vessel was aptly named—she was the largest U.S. ship afloat. After he had settled into his cabin, Rowland went to find the purser to ask him if he could hold a Sunday morning church service on board. To his surprise, the purser beat him to it. After introducing himself, the purser said, "I am wondering if you are the man I am looking for. I need a preacher to conduct our Sunday morning service."

"I must congratulate you, sir," Rowland replied. "In all my years of travel you are the first purser I have ever known to come looking for a preacher. I have had to start an argument with many a purser to get permission to preach. Of course, I would be delighted to preach."

On Sunday morning Rowland delivered a sermon based upon his lectures on fulfilled prophecy. Those who attended the service were so taken with the subject that they begged Rowland to deliver the message again, this time in front of more people. Rowland agreed to this, and that night a huge crowd gathered in the aft deck lounge to hear him speak. The following night they wanted to hear more, and so Rowland gave a follow-up address. Then, on the third night, as more people gathered to hear him speak, he gave an address on the conditions in Africa and the work of missionaries there.

When Rowland had finished speaking, one of the men in the audience rose to his feet. "Thank you, Reverend Bingham," he began. "I think I speak for everyone here when I say it is impossible not to be moved by what we have heard. I do not think we ought to go back to our cabins without taking action. My friend here and I will be glad, if anyone feels moved as I do, to accept gifts of money to pass on to our brother for his work in Africa."

Rowland did not know what to say. Here he was on an ocean liner preaching to a crowd who wanted to take up an offering for the Sudan Interior Mission. All he could think was that God worked in mysterious ways. A large sum of money was collected that night, and when he arrived in England, Rowland turned it over to the SIM branch there. The money was soon put to good use paying for the fares of several missionaries headed to Africa. However, none of this helped solve Rowland's personal money needs. Still, Rowland was not worried. He knew that God was in control of the situation, and he waited to see what would happen.

The local SIM branch in Great Britain had arranged a week-long speaking tour for Rowland around England, Wales, and Scotland. Along the way Rowland stayed with many friends and promoted missions work wherever he went. While he was on the tour, several people handed Rowland money in envelopes marked "for your personal use," and when Rowland totaled it up, he had enough money to pay for the next portion of his voyage.

When Rowland returned to London, a letter was waiting for him from the Nortons, old friends who served with the Belgium Gospel Mission. The Nortons had heard that Rowland was embarking on a round-the-world trip and urged him to visit them on his way. Although Belgium was out of the way, Rowland wanted to encourage his friends. He felt that he could not turn down the opportunity to visit them, even though he did not have the extra money to pay for the more complicated route he would have to take to pass through Belgium. He changed his trip plans so that instead of leaving England by ship for Egypt, he would travel overland across Europe, passing through Belgium, Paris, Rome, and Naples.

In Belgium the Nortons had arranged three full nights of speaking engagements for Rowland. Once again Rowland spoke of the needs of Africa and the wonderful things he had seen there on his last visit. At the close of the service on the last night, a man whom Rowland knew slightly invited him to his house for lunch the following day. Rowland accepted the invitation, as long as the man could get him to the train station by midafternoon.

Rowland arrived at the man's house just before noon the following day. After a delicious lunch, his host said, "Now, Mr. Bingham, I am the Lord's banker, and I feel He wants me to have a little hand in this tour you are taking around the world." With that he pulled out his checkbook and wrote a check for five hundred dollars. But that was not all. "You are going to Paris next?" the man asked.

Rowland nodded.

"Then I would like you to be my guest during your time there. Go to the Hotel Blanche, where I always stay when I am in Paris. Give them my name and tell them to charge your room to me. Ah, but you will also need money for France." The man pulled open a drawer in his desk and reached around for a wad of French banknotes. Without even counting them he handed them to Rowland and said, "Here, these will see you through France."

Rowland was overwhelmed. "Thank you," he said humbly. He recalled how he had hesitated in coming to Belgium because he did not have enough money, and now he had more than enough to get him on his way again.

After enjoyable stays in Paris and Rome, Rowland traveled on to Naples, Italy, where he had plenty of money to book a passage on the *Italia* for the trip across the Mediterranean Sea to Alexandria, Egypt. Once again, on the ship he held a service on Sunday morning, although the Italian purser did advertise it as a "Protestant mass." At the close of the service, a woman came up and introduced herself. Rowland had mentioned in the course of the service that he was going to visit Palestine, and the woman told him that her father was the president of the Jerusalem Chamber of Commerce. She insisted that Rowland stay with her parents while he was in Jerusalem.

After the ship docked in Alexandria, Rowland traveled on to Cairo, where he spent time sightseeing. He visited the pyramids and the Sphinx and made an excursion to Luxor to visit the Valley of the Kings.

When he arrived in Jerusalem, he stayed with the woman's parents and had a wonderful time finally seeing sights that he had, to that point, only read about in his Bible. He visited the Western Wall, the remnant of the old Jewish temple, Mount Zion, the Mount of Olives, Gethsemane, and Solomon's stables, and walked the Via Dolorosa, the route Jesus is supposed to have walked on His way to be crucified. While in Palestine he also visited the Jordan River and the Dead Sea before traveling on to Beirut. He took many photographs with which to illustrate his Bible talks.

In Beirut he booked a seat on a motorcar cavalcade traveling to Baghdad. It consisted of five Cadillac cars that wound their way through the desert sand dunes. They were the only cars on the "road"; everyone else was traveling by camel. Along the route they passed by the cave of Machpelah, where Abraham was buried, and farther along they passed Ur of the Chaldees, where he was born. As they passed these places, Rowland thought about Abraham and how God had told him he would be a blessing to the whole world if he had faith. Rowland prayed that he, too, might leave a legacy of faith and blessing through the work of the Sudan Interior Mission.

Once he reached Baghdad, Rowland visited the ruins of Babylon nearby and traveled to the coast, where he took another ship through the Persian Gulf and on to India.

India fascinated Rowland. Although he could see many parallels there to Africa and the Sudan, it was also a very different culture, with its own challenges for missionaries.

Finally, after a month of preaching in India, Rowland set out on the next leg of his journey. In Australia he visited Perth, Melbourne, Sydney, and Brisbane. Everywhere he went, Rowland received an enthusiastic welcome from the Australians. He talked with many Christians who were looking for a way to be missionaries in Africa. And he talked with like-minded Christians when he visited New Zealand. Aware now of such interest, he took steps toward establishing SIM branches in both countries before setting out on the final leg of his journey back to Canada.

On the return voyage, Rowland thought a lot about the eager Christians he had talked to in New Zealand and Australia. As a person who had journeyed from Canada to the South Pacific, he knew what a long and harrowing voyage it was. If missionaries were to go from New Zealand to Nigeria, they would have to make a similarly grueling trip crossing the ocean to the Cape of Good Hope and then sailing on up the west coast of Africa. How much easier it would be for them if they could just sail across the Indian Ocean to East Africa. It would also make it easier for members of the newly formed Australian and New Zealand branches of the mission to visit their missionaries in the field. Regrettably, SIM had nothing to offer them in East Africa, as it had not begun any work there, choosing instead to concentrate its efforts on Nigeria and the western side of the Sudan interior. As the ship made its way northward across the Pacific Ocean, Rowland began to pray that God would somehow open up a door for SIM to begin working in East Africa.

When he returned to Toronto, Rowland spent some time catching up on the editions of *The Evangelical Christian* that had been published while he was away. As he read, one article jumped out at him. It was about a new mission, called the Abyssinian Frontiers Mission, working in Ethiopia, East Africa. When Rowland learned that one of the founders of the mission, Dr. Tom Lambie, was on furlough on Long Island, New York, he set off as soon as he could for New York to speak with him.

Rowland liked Tom from the moment he shook hands with him. As the two men sat together in a hotel lobby, Tom told Rowland his story.

"I am a medical doctor, and I worked with the United Presbyterian Mission in the Egyptian Sudan," Tom began. "In 1919, during the great flu epidemic, one of the Ethiopian governors asked if I could come and work there. Since Ethiopia had been hit particularly hard by the sickness, the mission gave me permission to open its first mission station there. Two other men, Alfred Buxton and George Rhoad, joined me. We did our best in the terrible situation, and when the epidemic was over, I got to meet Ethiopia's regent, Haile Selassie."

As Tom spoke, Rowland felt excitement rising within. Somehow he knew that this story would one day be connected with SIM.

Tom continued. "Haile Selassie had heard of our work and was very eager to give us a hand. He helped with all the legal red tape required for building the first hospital in Ethiopia. I was the head doctor, and as wonderful as that was, I could not get the idea out of my head that God wanted me to go to the pagan tribes in southern Ethiopia, tribes that had never heard of Jesus Christ."

Rowland watched Tom's eyes light up as he said this.

"But the United Presbyterian Mission didn't see things the same way," Tom said. "They felt they had enough on their hands with the hospital. They had a point, but still I couldn't shake the idea that I was to go south. Eventually I told Alfred and George what I was feeling, and after a lot of prayer, the three of us agreed that we would start our own mission organization to work in southern Ethiopia. It hasn't been easy, though," he added. "The three of us are of one mind, but there is so much logistical work to be done at home, and we have not found an effective way to recruit more missionaries."

Rowland reached out and grabbed Tom's arm. "I am sure the Lord has brought us together for the purpose of serving each other. Let's both go back to our missions and see if we can get everyone together for a meeting."

As Rowland left the hotel, he marveled at the wonderful timing of his meeting with Tom, and he felt sure that within a year or two the two missions would be helping each other.

Meanwhile Rowland had yet another project he turned his energy toward. This one involved an idea he had seen work in England. Since 1875, English, Scottish, and Irish Christians had held an interdenominational conference at Keswick, in the Lake District of England. Over the years this conference had become very well known, and many influential Christian leaders had spoken at it. Rowland decided that he would start a Keswick conference in Canada so that Canadian Christians could come together in the summer to worship and learn more about God. It was an ambitious project, but Rowland had made many friends through running the newspaper and speaking at missionary conferences around the country.

When Rowland wrote an article for *The Evangelical Christian* about the idea of starting a Canadian Keswick conference, donations flooded in, and he was able to form a board and buy a dilapidated old hotel situated on 130 acres of land in Muskoka, Ontario. It was a perfect spot to get away from the noise and bustle of the city, and in the summer of 1925, the first Keswick conference was held there. The conference was a great success, despite the fact that the tent everyone gathered in was brought down one night by a heavy storm.

Rowland made sure that the conference was a haven for all types of missionaries. He charged missionaries on furlough a reduced rate or no rate at all. If they were in financial need, he even gave them money to bless them as they went on their way.

It was a year before all the representatives of the Abyssinian Frontiers Mission and the Sudan Interior Mission were able to get together. They met at the Keswick conference grounds. Much to Rowland's delight, both groups were unanimous in deciding that the two missions should join together. The Abyssinian Frontiers Mission became a part of SIM, with Tom Lambie leading the work in Ethiopia and George Rhoad serving as his deputy. Alfred Buxton, who was the son-in-law of the famous English missionary C. T. Studd, became the director of the Sudan Interior Mission in Britain. The goal of this union was to spread the gospel message along the borders of Ethiopia. By Christmas that year, the first party of nine SIM missionaries, many of them from New Zealand and Australia, had begun the work.

Rowland followed events in Ethiopia very closely. It was often touch and go, as the missionaries were sometimes refused the work and building permits they needed to operate. On several occasions they were even ordered out of the country. Somehow they managed to keep going, all the while praying that God would help them get their message out.

In 1929 Rowland Bingham decided to visit the work in Ethiopia and see for himself what was going on there. As he pored over a map of Africa, he came to the conclusion that the best way to get there was by overland journey from Nigeria. That way he could visit many SIM stations along the way. It hardly registered that he would be traveling over three thousand miles through some of the harshest terrain on earth.

Chapter 12

Across Africa

On October 16, 1929, Rowland Bingham, along with twenty-one missionaries and two children destined for service in Africa, climbed aboard the SS *Baltic.* They were bound for Liverpool, en route to Lagos. Down in the hold of the ship was a 1929 Ford Model A station wagon, which Rowland was delivering to Guy Playfair, who had recently been appointed the first field director of SIM. The car was needed to visit the now 165 mission stations that dotted the African landscape.

Rowland planned to be away for nine months, and once more he left *The Evangelical Christian* in the capable hands of his wife. Additionally, both SIM and the Canadian Keswick conference had boards that were able to function without his constant attention.

As the ship finally approached Lagos and the red mud of the Niger River began to color the seawater, Rowland was grateful that soon he would be setting foot again in his beloved Africa. He could hardly wait to see for himself what had happened since his last visit. He could not have imagined just how strong some of the native churches had become in his absence.

One of the first places he visited was Egbe, where he had participated in the baptism of 111 Christians fifteen years before. Rowland was just in time for the annual Bible conference, which was held in Egbe's brand-new church building. The building was the sturdiest of its kind in the area. It even had an imported tin roof, which had been completely paid for by the thousand-strong congregation.

Tommie Titcombe explained that this was quite a feat, since the top wage for a day's labor was only ten cents for a man and five cents for a woman. And not only had they raised money for the roof, they had also raised $150 to pay for the printing of a Bible translation in one of the interior tribal languages.

Alex Banfield was also at Egbe to meet Rowland. He was the sole survivor of the group of four missionaries that came to Africa in 1901 and established SIM's first mission station at Patigi. He had seemed the least likely of the group to succeed, and Rowland had accepted him for service only because he had good mechanical abilities. Despite his lack of formal education, Alex proved to have tremendous ability in learning foreign languages. After he had served one term with SIM, the British and Foreign Bible Society had invited him to be their representative for all of West Africa. With Rowland's blessing he had accepted the position and was now responsible for much of the Bible translation work going on in Africa. He had single-handedly translated the entire Bible into the Nupe language. Rowland was very glad to see Alex again and to know that he had been used to do something much greater than he had ever imagined possible.

From Egbe Rowland moved on to visit Jos, farther to the northeast, where SIM operated the Niger Press. The press turned out portions of the Bible in thirty-five different languages. Rowland was pleased to see so much attention being given to the printed page. He believed it was one of the fastest ways to spread the gospel message, even into areas where missionaries were unwelcome.

Jos was also where Andrew Stirrett was now stationed, and Andrew and Rowland had a delightful reunion. At sixty-five Andrew was still going strong. He preached in the marketplace every day and was often pelted with stones or rotten vegetables for his effort. Undeterred, with a twinkle in his eye, he told Rowland that the work of God was growing and he had seen many marvelous conversions in the marketplace. Rowland was humbled to think that he had vacillated on accepting the doctor because of his age. Andrew may have been their oldest missionary candidate, but he had proved to have staying power. He still amazed missionaries half his age with the hardships he could endure.

One of the reasons Rowland had come to Jos at this time was to attend a meeting of leaders of all the missionary societies working in the area. The main topic on the agenda was how to penetrate the four northern Nigerian provinces of Sokoto, Kano, Katsina, and Bornu. Together these areas represented nine million people. The Muslim leaders would not allow any Christian missionaries in this region, and although the British government had the right to overrule them, it chose not to do so. This stand had infuriated Rowland for some time because, in theory, all people living in British territories and protectorates had the right to freedom of religion, although practice was proving quite different from theory.

Everyone at the meeting sympathized with Rowland's frustration, but nobody knew what to do about it. Finally, Rowland got tired of hearing them go around and around the same topic. He stood up and said, "Friends, we have talked endlessly about how to open up the Muslim areas to the north, but we have been unable to come up with any plans to do so. Unless something very definite is decided upon here, I am going to go to Kano City as soon as this meeting is over. There I will stand in the marketplace and preach the gospel to the people. I know this may seem an extreme action to take, especially since I will probably be imprisoned, but something needs to be done to draw attention to the fact that there is no religious liberty in that area."

As he sat down, Rowland looked around at the stern faces of the other missionary leaders. One of the leaders hastily stood up and spoke.

"Now, perhaps Reverend Bingham is right. We have all sat back too long and bemoaned the fact that the northern districts are unjustly closed to us. Maybe it is time to take some real action. I for one do not want the good reverend to be arrested, so I propose that we go directly from this meeting to see the governor of Nigeria and ask him to approach the colonial secretary in London so that something can be done. Will that satisfy you, Reverend Bingham?"

Rowland nodded. "I am quite sure that the average British citizen has no idea of the stranglehold the Muslim leaders have over the gospel here. It is a disgrace to our country. Let us all pray that the meeting will be a success and that we can all work freely in the north soon."

Rowland determined to do more than pray, however. He wrote a note in his journal reminding himself to stop over in London on his way back to Canada and see what could be done about allowing Christians into the northern provinces. He was sure that if just one or two missionaries were allowed into each region, it would lead to a landslide of change for the people there.

Rowland's next stop was one that he was particularly looking forward to. Guy Playfair drove him from Jos in the Model A station wagon to visit the Tangale tribe.

What a difference fifteen years had made. Gordon Beacham and John Hall, the two missionaries who had come to the Tangale after hearing Rowland speak about them in Canada, were there to greet him. The two missionaries invited Rowland to speak to the church that Sunday night. They also apologized. "If you had been here this morning," they said, "you would have had fifteen hundred Tangale Christians to preach to. But tonight there will probably be only about eight or nine hundred in attendance. There are fewer at night because so many of our people like to go out on Sunday afternoon and evening and preach the gospel in the surrounding towns and villages, and so they miss the evening service."

Rowland was astounded at the number of Christians who attended the church. When he had visited the Tangale with Andrew Stirrett fifteen years before, they had been warned that it was life threatening to go among these people. Now the Tangale held out their arms to welcome him.

Rowland was not sure what message he should preach that night, so he asked John, "What should I speak about?"

"Anything you would speak of with your church at home," John replied. "Our people can understand it. We have translated the whole New Testament into their language and taught them to read it. Give them a missionary message; that's what you are all about, Reverend Bingham."

Rowland spoke that night to eight hundred people. The room was stiflingly hot, and his body ached from the rough roads they had driven over, but he was glad for the opportunity to challenge the Tangale Christians to continue going out to preach the gospel.

At the end of the service, the congregation insisted on taking up an offering for missionary work in other parts of Africa, and sixty-five dollars was given. What was more important, though, was that four of the best young men in the town came forward to volunteer to go as missionaries into the Muslim provinces to the north. The remainder of the church pledged to support them.

Rowland was thrilled. Here was a church that fifteen years ago did not exist taking up the call to missions. He could hardly wait to get to Ethiopia and share the same message there.

Soon it was time for Rowland to be on his way to Ethiopia. He made his way back to Jos, where Guy arrived to pick him up in the Ford station wagon. They set out on their journey on February 7, 1930. Henry Stock, another SIM missionary, accompanied them on the journey. The Ford was laden with provisions for the trip. A large box was tied to the left-hand running board for more storage, and their bedrolls were tied to the front fenders. Among the provisions they had to carry with them was gasoline. Since there would be few places along the way where they could purchase fuel, they needed to take an ample supply with them.

Two days after setting out, they arrived at Lake Chad, on the border between Nigeria and Chad. They camped for the night beside the lake. Lake Chad was alive with bird life, and Rowland watched as huge flocks of ducks, geese, pelicans, and other birds he had never seen before flew overhead and glided down to the water at the edge of the lake.

The next day the three men crossed a river near the village of Ngala on a pontoon made of empty gasoline cans set inside a wooden frame with a deck on top. To Rowland it hardly seemed substantial enough to carry the station wagon across the river. Despite sitting low in the water once the vehicle was driven onto it, somehow the pontoon carried them to the other side.

As the men made their way across Chad, they spent a night among the Sara people. The Sara were reputed to be the tallest people in Africa. The average height of the men was six feet two inches, and a number of men in the village were over six feet seven inches tall. The Sara women were also unique. They were called the "duckbilled" women because of the large wooden disks placed in their lips.

The men then drove west across a large plain covered with scrubby brush. Although driving on the plain was comparatively easy, even though the road was little more than a track, thorns slowed their progress. The large, spiky thorns punctured the tires, causing them to stop and make repairs at the side of the track.

On February 20 the men reached Monga and entered the Belgian Congo. They drove on to the town of Bouta, a large commercial center in the heart of Africa where, to their surprise, they discovered a Ford dealership and garage. Here they were able to replenish their gasoline supply before moving on.

Unlike when traveling over the plains in Chad, the men were now driving through dense jungle, with many rivers to cross. On one occasion they came to a river where again they had to be ferried across on a pontoon boat. This time, however, the ramps that allowed vehicles to drive on and off the ferry were poorly formed and muddy. Still, despite the treacherous approaches, Guy safely guided the Model A station wagon aboard and safely off on the other side of the river. As they drove away, Rowland looked back to see that a truck that had pulled up behind them had not fared as well. The truck, laden with goods, slid sideways on the muddy ramp and then rolled forward into the river, where it was soon completely submerged. The last thing Rowland saw as they rounded a corner and the scene faded from view was the driver of the truck standing knee-deep in water on the roof of his vehicle.

As they passed through the Belgian Congo, the men encountered a tribe of Pygmies. These people were about four and a half feet tall. Rowland marveled at the contrasts in Africa; on their trip they had seen probably the tallest and the shortest people in the world.

Eventually the men crossed into Uganda and came to the Nile River. Here they stopped and took a sixty-mile sightseeing cruise down the river on a steamer before heading on to Kampala, the capital of Uganda. After replenishing their supplies, they moved on again, crossing into Kenya. The roads in Kenya were wider, and the men were able to make better time on their journey—that is, until they entered the vast Rift Valley, which was alive with animals of all kinds. Elephants wandered nearby, as did rhinoceroses and lions, and for the first time on the journey, Rowland saw zebra, which roamed in great herds across the valley.

As Rowland took in the spectacular sight of so many animals, it began to rain. Soon the torrential rain began to turn the roads to mud. Before long the Model A was axle-deep in the mud.

Rowland and Henry stood drenched in the rain, pushing the station wagon as Guy sat behind the wheel and tried to guide it through the mud. On several occasions they had to jack the vehicle up and put pieces of wood and leaves beneath the wheels to try to free it. But in the end the road proved to be impassable, and the men left the car and traveled on to Nairobi by train. They arrived there on Saturday, March 8, a month after setting out from Jos, Nigeria. They had traversed the African continent, covering more than thirty-five hundred miles.

In Nairobi Rowland left Guy and Henry, who several days later set out on the return trip to

Nigeria. Because of the roads made impassable by the torrential rain, Rowland flew north in a small plane to Moyale, on Kenya's border with Ethiopia. There Tom Lambie, accompanied by George Rhoad, was awaiting his arrival. The two men were going to escort Rowland on a tour of the SIM mission stations in Ethiopia.

"Welcome to Ethiopia, Reverend Bingham," Tom said as Rowland stepped from the small plane. "The missionaries here have been eagerly awaiting your arrival. I trust your trip across the continent was enjoyable."

"Yes, enjoyable, interesting, and challenging," Rowland replied. "I have been eager to get to Ethiopia and see for myself the wonderful work I have been reading so much about in your letters."

"I don't think you will be disappointed," Tom replied.

The men spent the night in Moyale and set out the following morning. This time there was no Ford Model A station wagon to ride in. Instead Rowland climbed onto the back of a donkey for the journey north, while a group of porters carried their belongings. Rowland was impressed with the porters, who seemed to be able to effortlessly balance heavy loads on their heads.

The first mission station the men visited was located in the town of Homatcho, where two missionaries, Glen Cain and Eric Horn, were stationed. The mission station consisted of three huts, with more planned. The two missionaries were also busy learning the local language.

The group stayed in Homatcho overnight. In the morning, accompanied by Glen and Eric, they set out for the mission station at Soddu, to the northwest, where a mission conference of all the SIM missionaries serving in Ethiopia had been arranged.

As Rowland stood to address the conference on Monday, April 21, 1930, his eyes took in a wonderful sight. Before him were so many missionaries he had been praying for as they established the work of the Sudan Interior Mission in Ethiopia. Rowland told the group how proud he was of their efforts and then told them of all the wonderful things he had seen and experienced while visiting the SIM stations in Nigeria.

After Rowland's address, the conference got down to discussing a number of issues affecting the growth of the mission in Ethiopia. They talked about how to raise money for the new work and when it was appropriate to accept an offering.

Another issue they discussed was what stance the Sudan Interior Mission should take toward the Abyssinian Coptic Church, which was similar to the Greek Orthodox Church. Rowland had been studying the issue for some time. While much of the population of Ethiopia was not Christian and many had never even heard the gospel, the Coptic Church had existed in the country for centuries. Christianity had first come to Ethiopia seventeen hundred years before, when two Syrian boys were captured after their father's merchant ship was raided in the Red Sea. The two boys, who were both Christians, were brought back to Ethiopia and grew up to become court advisers to the king. They proclaimed the gospel to the king, who, along with his family, eventually became a Christian, which in turn led to the founding of the Abyssinian Coptic Church. Now the Coptic Church was not happy about Protestant missionary organizations working in the country. The church had put so much pressure on the government that the government was considering having all SIM missionaries expelled from Ethiopia.

After discussing the matter for some time, Rowland rose and addressed the group. "With regards to our relationship to the Abyssinian Coptic Church," he began, "our position should be that we undertake that we will not speak against the church. Our work will be positive and not negative, and therefore we will endeavor to speak the truth in love." Rowland was interested in making friends, not enemies, of fellow Christians, even if they did want SIM expelled.

After the conference Rowland visited the other two SIM mission stations in Ethiopia. Then he set out for the capital, Addis Ababa, where SIM planned to set up its administrative headquarters for Ethiopia. High mountains and lush vegetation surrounded the group on all sides as they made their way along. Despite the grand scenery, Rowland was glad to reach Addis Ababa so that he could finally climb off the bony donkey he had been riding all the way from the border with Kenya.

On May 24, several days after their arrival in Addis Ababa, Rowland and Tom went to the royal palace for an audience with Haile Selassie. Haile Selassie was due to be crowned emperor soon, and Rowland was anxious to gain his support for the mission. The two men set out for the palace with two Persian cats in closed baskets. The cats, which Tom had had one of his returning missionaries bring from London, were a gift for the ruler.

Haile Selassie, a short, slightly built man, gave the two missionaries an enthusiastic welcome. After he patted the two cats and handed them off to a servant, the men talked together. Rowland laid out all that SIM would like to do in the country. By the end of the meeting, he had secured the soon-to-be emperor's support. Haile Selassie was particularly interested in seeing the mission establish some medical work, especially among the numerous lepers in the country. Rowland agreed that this would be a good idea and promised to look into the possibility of a leper hospital.

"I believe that as a result of our meeting, the work of SIM in Ethiopia is secure. May God bless and guide our endeavors," Rowland said to Tom as they left the palace.

Tom nodded contemplatively as they began to wind their way through the maze of the capital's streets back to where they were staying.

Following the meeting with Haile Selassie, it was time for Rowland to begin the journey home. Tom was going to accompany Rowland on the trip. He was traveling back to the United States, where his wife, Charlotte, was recuperating from an illness.

The two men traveled to the coast and boarded a ship bound for London. Rowland had not forgotten the note he had written to himself during the conference in Jos, Nigeria. While in London he intended to visit government officials and see what could be done about letting missionaries into the four northern provinces of Nigeria.

As the ocean liner glided along, Rowland thought about all that he had seen in Ethiopia and wrote a letter of encouragement to the SIM missionaries he had met there. He was concerned that the missionaries not lose focus in their ministry by concentrating too much on building a mission bureaucracy, or "methods," as he called it, at the expense of ministering to the local people they had come to share the gospel with. Drawing from the Sudan Interior Mission's experience in Nigeria, he wrote:

> But let us not be concerned about our methods until, by thorough mastery of the language first, and then, through that channel, a careful entering into the thought of the people, we are in a position to wisely approach our great task of evangelism. Let there be faithful daily application to the

> thorough acquisition of these languages ere we assume judgement as to methods and manner of approach. Foundations are being laid and they must be carefully laid in a new land, and utmost deference must be given to the voice of experience in this sphere.
>
> Should God spare me to come again to this field, I look forward to meeting men and women with the closest linguistic contact with, and knowledge of, these people, which are the prerequisites to successful evangelism and true church building.

With the letter written, Rowland turned his attention to how he would plead his case for religious tolerance in Nigeria once he reached London.

Chapter 13

Everything Went Black

Upon his arrival in London in July 1930, Rowland learned that the governor of Nigeria had rejected the missionaries' joint plea to open up the Muslim areas in the north of the country. But Rowland was not prepared to take no as the final answer. He knew he had to do more, and so he made his way to the International Council of Missions headquarters. He arrived at just the right time. The chairman of the council, Dr. Oldham, informed Rowland that all the secretaries were meeting the following day, and although the agenda was full, he would give Rowland a few minutes to present his case and see if he could rouse any interest in the Nigerian situation.

The next day, just before Rowland was scheduled to speak to the council, a representative of the Church of England, Great Britain's official church, got up to speak about Africa. Rowland was shocked by his words.

"As for Nigeria," the representative said, "our mission finds that there are no serious problems there. All that is required is men who understand the way the government works there and who are used to dealing with matters of state."

As soon as he could, Rowland rose to his feet and spoke. "I have to take issue with your statement," he said in a very firm voice. "If government exclusion of Christian missionaries from vast millions of people who have no access to the gospel, and would not be able to embrace it if they heard it, is not a serious matter, then I don't know what is. Our missionaries, many of whom have been in Nigeria for twenty-five years or more and are well acquainted with the government, have tried every way to approach government officials about this problem. We have reached a place of desperation and are now prepared to challenge the things being done under the British flag as being absolutely opposite to what the British people are led to believe is happening. Again I emphasize, there are many millions of people who live in these regions who have no opportunity to hear the gospel preached. Something must be done about it!"

When he had finished speaking, Rowland sat down to see what would happen next. Would the

International Council stir to action, or would it accept the words of the Church of England's representative?

Dr. Oldham was the next person to speak. "I have to say that I must confirm all that Mr. Bingham states," he began. "The situation in Nigeria is intolerable. All I ask is that Mr. Bingham be patient, and we will do our utmost to convey to the foreign office the seriousness of the situation."

Rowland felt confident that Dr. Oldham understood the situation and was prepared to act, so he accepted his advice to be patient just a little longer.

Sure enough, within a few weeks of arriving back in Canada, Rowland heard that Dr. Oldham was going to Nigeria to meet with the governor himself. He was even more pleased when he got a letter from Dr. Oldham telling him that the governor of Nigeria had promised that the government would put pressure on the Muslim emirs in the north to embrace the principle of religious toleration and allow missionaries into their regions.

Within a few months, SIM and the other mission organizations were allowed to open mission stations in formerly forbidden areas. Rowland was pleased with the part he had played in making this possible. He looked forward to receiving good reports from the new stations that were opening up.

As usual, Helen had done a wonderful job running *The Evangelical Christian.* Rowland caught up on the issues that had been published in his absence, and then he wrote several articles for the paper about his recent exploits in Africa. He also gave the board of SIM a full report on his trip and brought them up to date on the work of the mission in both Nigeria and Ethiopia. And the Canadian Keswick conference was going strong. Rowland was soon busily involved organizing the details of the next conference as well as his daughter Marianne's wedding to Meredith Dallman, a Baptist minister.

Three years rolled by, and when Rowland learned that six new missionaries, including one of Helen's nieces, who was a registered nurse, would soon be departing for Ethiopia, he took it as an opportunity to accompany them. He was anxious to see firsthand again how SIM's work was progressing there.

Rowland arrived in Addis Ababa on February 6, 1934. A meeting of the Ethiopia field council was arranged for his first four days there. During the gathering it was decided that Rowland and Tom Lambie should go north to investigate the possibility of opening a mission station in Lalibella. The prospect of this new station had come as a surprise to the Sudan Interior Mission. The city was the center of worship for the Coptic Church, yet the governor of the province had requested SIM's presence. He had heard of the good work SIM was doing in the south, and he did not want the cities in his province to miss out on anything.

One of the missionaries, James Luckman, drove Rowland, Tom, and Tom's wife, Charlotte, over the Entoto Mountains by car. A mule caravan containing supplies had been sent on ahead five days before. The entire journey to Lalibella took three bone-jarring weeks, as they drove around the Blue Nile Gorge and zigzagged their way up and down steep canyons.

When they arrived in Lalibella, Hiruy, the head priest of the Coptic Church, personally welcomed them and showed them some of the stunning sights of the area. The most impressive were the twelve churches carved out of sandstone rock. Rowland had never seen anything quite like it. The churches sat below ground level, where they had been carved out of the sandstone rock, with steps descending down into them. From inside they looked like an ordinary church, except the floor was twenty feet below ground and the whole church was one piece of rock.

The governor of Lalibella even sent a messenger to show Rowland and Tom several suitable building sites and allowed them to pick out the one they preferred. Rowland could hardly believe how well everything was going, especially when the governor suggested they also plant a mission station farther north and start a school for the blind in another town, called Debre Markos. He took notes each day, outlining the favor SIM had found with the governor so that he could write about it in *The Evangelical Christian* when he returned to Canada.

Just as the missionaries were ready to start the long journey home, Charlotte Lambie became ill. Tom told Rowland that it was serious and that he needed to get her back to Addis Ababa quickly and onto the correct course of medication. The governor offered them the use of his radio transmitter. Tom was able to get a call through to Emperor Haile Selassie's secretary, who readily agreed to send the emperor's private airplane to pick up Charlotte and bring her back to the capital.

When the plane arrived, it had enough room for Tom and Rowland to go along as well. As a result Rowland got a panoramic view of the land they had driven over. The rugged mountains were impressive, and Rowland could easily see why it had taken them three weeks to drive the same distance it took only an hour and twenty minutes to fly. Right there and then, Rowland decided that one day SIM would have airplanes of its own to help in emergencies and save "wear and tear" on the missionaries.

Charlotte Lambie made a swift recovery once she started her treatment in Addis Ababa.

Since he had flown back from Lalibella, Rowland had three weeks to spare. He decided to head south to Soddu, where several of the new missionaries had been sent. This brought the total number of SIM missionaries in that town to sixteen, and Rowland knew they could do with some encouragement. Much as in the early days of the work in Nigeria, the missionaries had seen little in the way of results from their work—barely one convert apiece, in fact.

Rowland spent a week in Soddu, conducting Bible studies and praying with the workers. He reassured them that many people around the world were praying for them and that a breakthrough would happen soon. What he did not know was that things were about to get a lot worse for the missionaries.

By April 1934 Rowland was back in Canada receiving weekly reports from Tom, who was becoming increasingly alarmed about the actions of Benito Mussolini, the dictator who had taken over Italy. It seemed that Mussolini was not content to have control of Eritrea, on Ethiopia's northern border. He had set his sights on taking over Ethiopia as he attempted to establish a new "Roman Empire."

As a totalitarian ruler, Mussolini wanted to be in total control of everything his subjects said and did, and Christianity was not an approved activity. The thought of Mussolini's conquering Ethiopia sent Rowland and the other SIM workers to their knees. Rowland knew that SIM did not have a strong hold in Ethiopia. Despite an influx of dedicated new missionaries, SIM had seen the conversion and baptism of only sixty-two Ethiopians. The door had opened only a crack, and Rowland longed to see it flung wide open.

At the end of May 1935, just as Rowland was worrying about the SIM missionaries and their converts in Ethiopia, he was asked to speak at a large rally in London, Ontario. Following the last meeting of the rally, as Helen drove Rowland back to the home where they were staying, a car coming in the opposite direction crossed the center line and careened head-on into them. Rowland barely knew what had happened before he found himself being catapulted through the windshield. Then everything went black.

Rowland awoke two days later in a hospital bed. A nurse walked past him, but when he tried to call out to her, he could not open his mouth—it was wired shut. Later that day he found out that the accident had fractured his jaw, several ribs, and his pelvis and left many deep cuts on his arms and legs. Helen was in a similar, serious condition. Their predicament was made all the worse because they were now both in their sixties.

Gradually Rowland's and Helen's bones and wounds began to heal, though it was a year before Rowland could get around without a walking stick. Still, in a letter to a close friend, he wrote,

> I was thrown through the windscreen, and yet both my eyes were spared injuries, and today I want this to be a word of gratitude and real thanksgiving to God.... Now I find my former vigor almost fully restored and a greater program than ever before me. I can only conclude that I have not yet finished the work of fulfilling the purpose for which the Lord Jesus laid hold upon me nearly fifty years ago when in His infinite mercy He saved me.

In June 1935 Tom visited "home," though he could no longer legally call the United States home. He had given up his American citizenship to become an Ethiopian citizen. When he visited Rowland, still in the hospital recovering, he explained that he had become an Ethiopian citizen to make it easier for SIM to negotiate to buy property in the country. Despite his injuries, Rowland was once again impressed by the sacrifice of his workers.

Tom confided to Rowland that he had been to see the emperor just before he left and that Haile Selassie felt certain that Italy was on the brink of invading his country. On the strength of this prediction, Tom had already applied to the Red Cross to start a division in Ethiopia so that they could be ready for the casualties of war. In fact, he had just visited the Red Cross international headquarters in Switzerland to beg them to make preparations so that they might be ready to meet the need when the war came, but he could not rouse any interest. They told him that it was their job to respond to wars and other disasters, not to anticipate them.

By August Rowland was sure that an invasion of Ethiopia was coming soon, and he did whatever he could to help the missionaries brace for what lay ahead. He was barely well enough to travel, but he insisted on going to a medical supply house in New York City. He ordered hospital beds and an operating table, which he had shipped on the first available vessel to Percy Roberts in Ethiopia. Dr. Roberts had set up a small hospital in Soddu. Rowland also collected as many packets of seed as he could and sent them to the various mission stations. If the Italians cut off the food supply, at least the missionaries would be able to grow some food for themselves.

On October 3, 1935, Rowland listened to the grim news on the radio. Mussolini had ordered his Italian troops to cross the Mareb River and invade Ethiopia. Soon reports came from Tom that all the foreign consulates had been closed and diplomats were leaving. In addition, the United States and British governments had ordered all their citizens in Ethiopia to evacuate immediately. Tom wanted to know what to tell the eighty SIM workers in the country.

Rowland was well aware that if the SIM doctors and nurses left the country, there would be no more than a dozen doctors and up to twenty nurses in all of Ethiopia. Ethiopia needed missionaries as never before, yet these men and women would be in great danger if they stayed. After much prayer, Rowland sent a telegram to Tom that read, "You are under higher orders than those of the King of England or the President of the United States. Get your instructions from Him and we are right with you. We approve of the sending home of mothers with children who cannot help."

Word soon came back that all the SIM missionaries had decided to stay and throw in their lot with the Ethiopian people, whatever it cost them.

The Italian forces soon ordered Western missionaries out of the northern areas of the country, though the Red Cross was allowed to advance to the battlefields. As a result many SIM workers changed roles and went north with the Red Cross mule trains, sharing the gospel message as they went.

Very few letters came from Ethiopia now, and those that did arrive were smuggled across the border and sent from Kenya. The letters told horrific stories of a country in turmoil. Not only had the Italian troops invaded the country but also many of the small tribes had taken advantage of the turmoil to launch their own "mini wars" against their enemies around the country.

Eventually there was a complete blackout of news from Ethiopia; even the letters that had been smuggled to Kenya and mailed stopped coming. Rowland, along with the Canadian support staff of SIM, waited anxiously to hear what was happening.

The next news they heard came over the radio. The report stated that Emperor Haile Selassie had fled Ethiopia and was on his way to England. Rowland made immediate plans to visit him there.

Chapter 14

A Little Faith in a Great God

Haile Selassie welcomed Rowland into his house in Bath, England. It was a sad moment for Rowland to see the emperor, who had helped SIM so much, now in exile with his family. And the things that Haile Selassie told him about his recent trip to the League of Nations headquarters in Switzerland angered Rowland.

Haile Selassie told Rowland that he went to a session of the League of Nations to ask for help in driving the Italians out of Ethiopia. Since Ethiopia had been a member of the League since 1923, he hoped that the other members would be able to do something to help his country. But no one was particularly interested in the invasion of Ethiopia by Mussolini. Many of the countries in the League had colonies in Africa themselves, and they did not see any great harm in Italy's expanding her colonies from Eritrea southward to the formerly independent Ethiopia. Besides, their attention was taken up trying to keep peace in Europe as Adolf Hitler and his National Socialist Party were gaining strength. Many representatives at the League of Nations believed that if Mussolini were allowed to stay in Ethiopia, he would be less likely to ally with Hitler and pose an even bigger threat to the rest of Europe.

Haile Selassie was devastated by the League of Nations' callousness and lack of respect for their own covenant, which promised that one country in the League could count on the others to come to its rescue if it were attacked. In summing up the situation, Haile Selassie told Rowland the warning he had given to the League of Nations when it became clear it would not help his country. He had said, "I did not think that fifty-two nations, among them the greatest powers in the world, could be defeated by one aggressor. God and history will remember your judgment. If you do not come to the aid of a weak fellow member, then who will be next to fall?"

There was little Rowland could say in defense of England or the other members of the League of Nations. Like Haile Selassie, he felt that they had let Ethiopia down, and he wondered which country Mussolini would set his sights on next. All he could do was tell the emperor that many Christians around the world were praying for him to return to

Ethiopia, even though at the moment the chances of that happening seemed slim.

Soon after visiting Haile Selassie, Rowland read in the newspaper that most of the members of the League of Nations had recognized Italy's sovereignty over Ethiopia, which the conquerors had merged with Eritrea and Somaliland to form Italian East Africa. The words of the emperor rang in Rowland's ears. "If you do not come to the aid of a weak fellow member, then who will be next to fall?"

Rowland kept the cause of the Italian occupation of Ethiopia before Christians around the world through articles in *The Christian Evangelical* and through his many speaking engagements.

Before long Rowland found that he had to take another trip to Nigeria. This was because the government of the country had approached the Sudan Interior Mission and asked if it would be interested in taking over three leper hospitals it ran in the northern provinces. This was a most unusual request, since the government was still not eager to encourage missions in the north. It was even more unusual when the government offered to partner with SIM and pay one quarter of the costs of running the three hospitals. Rowland saw this as a wonderful opportunity to spread the gospel message northward and help the lepers, who often suffered greatly. Many leprosy patients stayed in the hospital for years before their condition was stabilized by the medicines or they died from their disease.

Rowland wanted to go to Nigeria with a definite answer for the government, but he knew that three hospitals would take a lot of money to run. Before he left, he approached the American Leprosy Mission to see if it would help with the expenses. It offered to pay 20 percent of the operating costs, and that, combined with the 25 percent the government was prepared to contribute, left SIM to come up with 55 percent of the funds. Could they do it? The more Rowland prayed, the more convinced he became that this was the next step God had for the mission. He set off for Nigeria to complete negotiations on the transfer of the hospitals.

Everything went smoothly, and Rowland set out from Lagos in a Ford V-8 sedan to see the three new hospitals, one near Sokoto and two near Kano. Traveling with him were three nurses and Dr. Albert Hessler, a veteran missionary who had volunteered to supervise the running of the hospitals.

When Rowland reached Minna, about 350 miles from the coast, he felt ill and was soon sent to bed. The following morning Albert urged him to stay in bed and rest, but Rowland wanted to keep going. He was determined to cover the remaining three hundred miles to the hospital in Sokoto that day.

"I don't want to hold anyone up," Rowland told Albert, "but I must admit I would feel better if I could just nibble on some unsalted almonds. I do believe they would settle my stomach."

Albert shook his head. "I am sorry," he said, "but I have been in Nigeria for fifteen years, and I have never seen anything but a few *salted* almonds, brought in by English people for Christmas. And it is a long time after Christmas now."

"I still think they would do me good. Would you mind going out to the nearest shop and seeing if they might by chance have some?" Rowland asked.

The doctor agreed and left Rowland to pack his clothes. He returned twenty minutes later with a look of wonderment on his face.

"You'll never guess what happened!" Albert exclaimed. "I asked the shopkeeper for almonds, and he said that he had just received a shipment of them. He told me he had never had them before, had no idea who would want to buy them, and he would never order them again. And they are unsalted!"

Rowland said a quick prayer of thanks as they climbed into the Ford and headed off on their way north. The almonds, which Rowland nibbled on all the way, kept his stomach settled as they traversed the deeply rutted roads.

As they neared Sokoto, Rowland said, "I wonder if they would have any tins of chocolate milk here."

"We are not in North America," Albert chuckled, "though when we get to the Sokoto station, I am sure someone could mix some chocolate in a glass of powdered milk for you."

"No," Rowland replied, pointing to a small shop ahead. "I have an idea that they might have some tins of chocolate milk in that shop, and I could drink it right away. Will you stop and see?"

Albert obediently pulled over, though from the look on his face, Rowland could see that he thought the idea of chocolate milk in Sokoto far-fetched. The two men got out of the vehicle and walked into the shop.

"Do you have any chocolate milk?" Albert asked.

The shopkeeper frowned. "No, we never have anything like that here," he said.

Rowland was surprised by his answer. He felt sure that there was chocolate milk somewhere in the store. They had just stepped out of the door when the shopkeeper called them back.

"Now that I think of it, there is a box in the back of my shop that came by mistake. I haven't opened it because I was going to return it, but it did say something about chocolate milk on the outside."

Sure enough, it was an entire case of chocolate milk imported from the United States. Once again Rowland thanked God for supplying all his needs, even in the middle of Nigeria.

Once they reached the hospital in Sokoto, Rowland and his companions ran into a problem. Many of the leprosy patients were scared of the five white people who had come to take over the hospital. Wild rumors circulated that these white people wanted to feed them good food to fatten them up and then kill them and boil them down for grease. Some of the lepers were so terrified that they fled, while others who were not mobile watched with great suspicion every move the doctor and nurses made.

Rowland sympathized with them. They had been cut off from the rest of the world for so long that they had no way of knowing what the truth was. And their Muslim leaders had obviously not prepared them to expect kindness from people of other religions.

Soon a number of the runaways returned, while other leprosy patients arrived to take the places of those who did not return, until the hospital was once again full.

Rowland also visited the two hospitals in Kano, and when things were running smoothly with the hospitals, he returned to Canada to shore up the work there.

Later, in August 1938, the last SIM missionaries were forced to leave Ethiopia. The Italians no longer allowed the Red Cross to have a presence in the country. The news saddened Rowland.

Then, a year later, on September 3, 1939, the world awoke to the news that Adolf Hitler had sent troops to invade Poland. As a result Britain and France declared war on Germany. Few people were shocked by this turn of events, as Hitler had been building an aggressive army for some time.

Rowland knew that Canada, as part of the British Empire, would soon be calling up young men for military service in Europe. He began to pray about how he could reach these young men with the gospel in such uncertain times. From his experiences in World War I, he knew that many of those called up would die on the battlefield while many others would suffer permanent injuries.

Within a month Rowland was inspired with an idea. What if he were to set up a network of cabins near the boot camps, where Christian soldiers could come for Bible study and fellowship and bring their non-Christian friends to hear the gospel message? Rowland discussed the idea with Helen. She was just as enthusiastic about it as he was, and the two of them set about making it happen.

The fact that it was yet another ministry that had no ongoing financial backing did not worry either of them. Rowland often told people that he did not have a great deal of faith, but that he had a little faith in a great God, and that great God would not let His causes fail.

Rowland called the new organization the Soldiers' and Airmen's Christian Association, or S.A.C.A. for short. The idea spread quickly with the help of exposure in *The Evangelical Christian* as well as through Rowland's hundreds of Christian connections around the country.

Plans moved swiftly, and somehow sixty-seven-year-old Rowland Bingham managed to find time for all of his various ministries. He prayed many times a day for the missionaries out in the field in Nigeria and the few Christians in Ethiopia.

As Rowland sat listening to the BBC news on the radio on May 13, 1940, he heard a recording of a speech the new prime minister of England, Winston Churchill, had delivered to the House of Commons. Churchill's voice boomed through the radio and filled the room. "I have nothing to offer the nation but blood, toil, tears, and sweat," he said. "We have before us an ordeal of the most grievous kind. We have before us many long months of struggle and suffering. You ask, what is our policy? It is to wage war against a monstrous tyranny, never surpassed in the dark, lamentable catalog of human crime. This is our policy. You ask, what is our aim? I can answer in one word: victory."

Rowland bought a copy of the newspaper that night and copied out the words of the speech into a notebook. They were exactly what he needed to encourage the SIM missionaries. As their leader, Rowland knew he could not offer them protection or ideal conditions to work in, especially during a global war. He knew that some of them might be called to lay down their lives. But he was convinced that the war years must not become an excuse for missionaries to retreat from their work. They must press on and take advantage of every situation to spread the good news of victory in Jesus Christ.

The following month, on June 10, 1940, as German troops advanced toward Paris, Italy joined Germany and Japan and declared war on France and Great Britain. Now that Italy was the enemy, Allied forces began targeting Italian East Africa, and another front was opened up in the war.

A month later Rowland received a letter saying that Haile Selassie was headed to the Anglo-Egyptian Sudan to lead Ethiopian troops who, along with the British, were going to try to take back Ethiopia from Mussolini.

With a new front in the war opening up in Africa, the seas became even more dangerous. Few passenger ships would travel through the Atlantic Ocean, which was patrolled by German U-boats that attacked any allied ship. This posed a problem for SIM in how to get both new missionaries and those returning from furlough to Nigeria. A few were sent to Tangier by ship and then across the desert to Nigeria by bus, but this was a long and arduous route and often took months to recover from. Deciding that something had to be done about it, Rowland chartered an Egyptian ship to take missionaries to Africa. In typical style he offered berths to other mission societies as well.

In December 1940 the ship with seventy-two missionaries on board set out for Lagos. Rowland was at the dock in New York City to see it off. After two anxious weeks, he received a telegram that the ship had arrived unharmed, though the missionaries were having difficulty finding beds in Lagos because all the available beds were filled with sailors who had been rescued from ships sunk by U-boats off the coast of Africa.

With that same attitude of finding a way to get things done, the work of S.A.C.A. was soon established. Within a year of the war's starting, Rowland had rented or built sixteen Christian fellowship cabins, each one permanently manned by an evangelist, pastor, or returned SIM missionary. The cabins soon attracted thousands of young soldiers and airmen, and word of them spread far and wide, especially after the governor general of Canada became the patron of S.A.C.A.

In addition to carrying out all his other responsibilities, Rowland found time to visit the cabins and encourage the workers. One of the first cabins he stopped at was in Halifax, Nova Scotia, where he had first landed in Canada fifty-three years before. The Canadian army, navy, and air force all had training camps in Halifax, and the S.A.C.A. workers reached out to them all. Bob Munro, who had been an SIM missionary for seventeen years, headed the work, assisted by Dick Oliver. Both of these men were Scots and World War I veterans who related easily to the young men preparing for combat.

Rowland was delighted to see how busy the cabin at Halifax was. A no-nonsense atmosphere prevailed as hundreds of young men came through the doors for Bible studies, counseling, and prayer. Some of the men had been Christians since childhood, but many of them had never set foot in a church before. All of them received a warm welcome and a sympathetic ear. Soon the testimonies of many of the young men found their way into *The Christian Evangelical,* encouraging many people around the world to pray for the troops in combat.

In January 1941 a combined Allied force began pushing the Italians out of Ethiopia. The Allies met little serious resistance, and on May 5 Rowland heard the great news on a BBC news report. The British and Ethiopian troops had fought their way through to the capital, and Haile Selassie was marching triumphantly back to Addis Ababa, nearly five years to the day since he had fled Ethiopia. Rowland was delighted to report in the next issue of *The Evangelical Christian* that the prayers of many Christians had been answered—Ethiopia had been liberated.

But there was even better news to follow. Laurie Davison, one of the SIM missionaries who had been called up to fight in the British army, was in the battalion that marched into the newly liberated capital city. Soon Rowland received a letter from Laurie reporting how elders from SIM's former mission station at Wallamo had trekked up to the capital to talk with him. The letter read:

> Now comes the astonishing news that there are over seventy groups of believers meeting regularly for worship. In the Sidamo province Ganami has proved a faithful pastor to his flock. Ato Biru, the leading evangelist in the Wallamo area, has done a truly splendid work. He spends his time walking around the province, telling out the gospel, teaching the young Christians and preparing them for baptism.
>
> When we left Ethiopia we had only three partly organized churches with no more than a hundred and fifty believers, but during the Italian occupation the numbers have grown in leaps and bounds, so that estimations are that there are now ten thousand believers!

Rowland had to agree with Laurie that it was truly astonishing news. While they had feared for the safety of the few Ethiopian Christians, those Christians had taken all that the missionaries had taught them about the Word of God and had applied it with wonderful results.

As the months rolled by, Rowland heard many stories about the faith and courage of the Ethiopian Christians. The jails seemed to have been particularly effective in spreading Christianity! Many Christians were imprisoned for continuing to preach and gather for prayer and worship while under Italian occupation. The jails were primitive, and in many cases the prisoners were not fed. Food had to be brought to them from the outside by friends and relatives.

The imprisoned Christians were cared for by their fellow believers and were brought enough food to meet not only their own needs but also the needs of others around them. This impressed the other prisoners, who wondered what kind of religion made people care so much for each other, and even for strangers. Many of them were converted as a result of this. Sometimes a prison warden would let the Christians go because they were creating too many converts in the prison. The wardens feared that if the Christians stayed any longer, the entire prison would be turned into one long prayer and preaching service!

The Italian governor of the province around Wallamo had also unwittingly played a part in spreading the gospel. In July 1939 the governor, determined to impress the Ethiopians under his rule, had ordered that a huge military parade be held in the town of Soddu. He then ordered that every man in the province attend the parade. Trucks were sent out to gather up the men and bring them the long distances to Soddu from their tribal areas.

Knowing that they would be severely beaten if they did not attend, the men from all the tribes in the area gathered to marvel at the Italian soldiers, tanks, and artillery on display. But when the show of force was over, the governor did not authorize the trucks to take the men home again. Instead the men were left to find their own way home as best they could. The Christians of Wallamo opened their homes to these men and told them about their faith and how it was stronger than any show of force they had seen from the Italians.

Hundreds of tribal men then returned to their tribes, taking the gospel message with them. Over time the elders from Wallamo visited them all, helping them to establish churches for the thousands of converts.

After the liberation of Ethiopia, SIM missionaries slowly returned to their former stations. Rowland published many amazing stories of events in Ethiopia in *The Christian Evangelical.* Eager to meet these new believers, he started making plans to visit Ethiopia. This was a long, involved process, with World War II still in progress, but he hoped to have all the details taken care of so that he could be in Ethiopia for Christmas 1942. How wonderful it would be to greet all the new Christians and meet with Haile Selassie back in his own country once again.

Chapter 15

Whose Faith Follow

Rowland and Helen Bingham spent the summer of 1942 at the Canadian Keswick conference grounds. Between preaching and speaking about missions, Rowland worked to finish the book he was writing for the Sudan Interior Mission's Fiftieth Jubilee. He had decided to title the book *Seven Sevens of Years and a Jubilee,* since seven times seven was forty-nine years, and the next year was the fiftieth. He had already written much of the history of the mission, dividing it into seven-year periods.

As he spent the afternoons outside his cabin, seated in the shade of tall, white birch trees, Rowland thought back to the early years. How long ago it seemed now when, as a young man of twenty, he had gone out to Africa with Walter

Gowans and Thomas Kent. The men had had little support behind them, but they were driven by the conviction that millions of people in the Sudan needed to hear the gospel. And now, as SIM stood on the brink of its fiftieth year, so much had been accomplished. SIM mission stations now dotted the African interior, and 360 missionaries served in the field. To support its missionaries, SIM collected and dispersed $400,000 a year.

But Rowland was never a man to be content with what had been done. He always saw the open doors ahead, and with Mussolini and the Italian forces now out of Ethiopia, he hoped for a bright future for that country. There was much to be done and, as usual, not enough workers.

As he put the finishing touches to *Seven Sevens of Years and a Jubilee,* Rowland did what he had done consistently for fifty years—he challenged both missionaries and Christians at home to evaluate how much they were doing to spread the gospel message around the world. The last words of the manuscript read:

> We are asking that in this Jubilee year of the Sudan Interior Mission our friends, as well as our missionaries, may recognize anew God's absolute right to all that we have and are. Only thus shall we be able to keep this Jubilee as unto the Lord and enter the "promised land."

The manuscript was 130 pages long—not nearly long enough to tell all the amazing things that Rowland had seen in Africa over the years. Rowland hoped that in spite of this, the book would give enough information to inspire young people to go out as missionaries. Because he wanted the book to reach as wide an audience as possible, he chose to have it bound in heavy paper instead of the usual hard cover. That way he could keep production costs to a minimum and produce more copies. By November 27 the manuscript was ready for publication by Evangelical Publishers in Toronto.

With the book out of the way, Rowland once again set his sights on traveling to Ethiopia for Christmas. He planned to leave on December 19, the date of his seventieth birthday. This time he planned to use a new method of transportation to get to Africa—a commercial aircraft. Although arranging such a flight during wartime had been a struggle, everything had finally come together to make it happen. Rowland desperately wanted to see the new mission stations in the country for himself and visit Haile Selassie to find out how SIM could help get Ethiopia back on its feet after such a devastating war.

Before he could leave, however, Rowland had a lot of paperwork that needed to be taken care of. On Friday morning, December 4, he went upstairs to his office to work. Just before lunch he was discovered in his office in a semiconscious state. Several people rushed to his aid, including Helen and their two daughters, Winifred and Marianne, who had been home helping their father with the final preparation of the manuscript for his book.

Rowland was carried to his bed, and a doctor was called. The diagnosis was concise. Rowland had suffered a massive stroke while working at his desk. For an hour or so he appeared to be improving, but then he slipped into unconsciousness. Nevertheless the doctor felt that there was a good chance that Rowland would recover.

Word was sent out to thousands of people around the world to pray for Rowland's recovery. But it was not to be. On Tuesday, December 8, 1942, Helen, Winifred, Marianne, and a group of faithful missionary friends, including Tom Lambie and Guy Playfair, gathered around Rowland Bingham's bed as he breathed his last.

When news of Rowland's death was made public, telegrams of condolence poured in from around the globe. It seemed there was not a single region on earth that Rowland's faith had not touched through either the Canadian Keswick conference, Evangelical Publishers, *The Evangelical Christian*, the Soldiers' and Airmen's Christian Association, or the work of the Sudan Interior Mission. Many expressed their admiration and debt to the one man who had carried the vision and weight of all five of these ministries.

The funeral service for Rowland Victor Bingham was held on December 10, 1942, at Cooke's Presbyterian Church in Toronto. The church was selected because it had the largest church auditorium in the city. The minister who conducted the service was Dr. P. W. Philpott, whom Rowland first met in 1889 when attending the Salvation Army in Halifax soon after his arrival in Canada. Like so many hundreds of other people, Dr. Philpott had become a lifelong friend and supporter of Rowland's many Christian endeavors.

The order of service, handed out to all those who attended the funeral, ended with these words:

> And so, for the first time, we face a New Year without him. Throughout his worldwide ministry—for he visited many lands—it was ever his joy to speak of God's great heroes, exhorting us to "imitate their faith"; and now that he, too, has joined that "great cloud of witnesses," we say one to another with new meaning as we remember him, "Rowland V. Bingham—Whose Faith Follow."

A few days after Rowland Bingham's funeral, the 360 SIM workers in Africa received their leader's annual Christmas newsletter, which Rowland had written and mailed out days before he died. Many of those who received the newsletter broke down and wept as they read Rowland's final message to them. Among them was Andrew Stirrett, who at seventy-seven years of age still preached every day in the marketplace at Jos.

Bibliography

Bingham, Rowland V. *Seven Sevens of Years and a Jubilee.* Evangelical Publishers, 1943.

Cotterell, F. Peter. *Born at Midnight.* Moody Press, 1973.

de la Haye, Sophie. *Tread Upon the Lion: The Story of Tommie Titcombe.* Sudan Interior Mission, 1974.

Hunter, J. H. *A Flame of Fire: The Life and Work of R. V. Bingham, D.D.* Sudan Interior Mission, 1961.

Percy, Douglas C. *Stirrett of the Sudan: The Beloved Physician of the Sudan.* Sudan Interior Mission, 1948.

Additional material from the SIM Archives, Charlotte, North Carolina.

About the Authors

Janet and Geoff Benge are a husband and wife writing team with more than thirty years of writing experience. Janet is a former elementary school teacher. Geoff holds a degree in history. Originally from New Zealand, the Benges spent ten years serving with Youth With A Mission. They have two daughters, Laura and Shannon, and an adopted son, Lito. They make their home in the Orlando, Florida, area.

Also from Janet and Geoff Benge...

More adventure-filled biographies for ages 10 to 100!

Christian Heroes: Then and Now

Gladys Aylward: The Adventure of a Lifetime • 978-1-57658-019-6
Nate Saint: On a Wing and a Prayer • 978-1-57658-017-2
Hudson Taylor: Deep in the Heart of China • 978-1-57658-016-5
Amy Carmichael: Rescuer of Precious Gems • 978-1-57658-018-9
Eric Liddell: Something Greater Than Gold • 978-1-57658-137-7
Corrie ten Boom: Keeper of the Angels' Den • 978-1-57658-136-0
William Carey: Obliged to Go • 978-1-57658-147-6
George Müller: Guardian of Bristol's Orphans • 978-1-57658-145-2
Jim Elliot: One Great Purpose • 978-1-57658-146-9
Mary Slessor: Forward into Calabar • 978-1-57658-148-3
David Livingstone: Africa's Trailblazer • 978-1-57658-153-7
Betty Greene: Wings to Serve • 978-1-57658-152-0
Adoniram Judson: Bound for Burma • 978-1-57658-161-2
Cameron Townsend: Good News in Every Language • 978-1-57658-164-3
Jonathan Goforth: An Open Door in China • 978-1-57658-174-2
Lottie Moon: Giving Her All for China • 978-1-57658-188-9
John Williams: Messenger of Peace • 978-1-57658-256-5
William Booth: Soup, Soap, and Salvation • 978-1-57658-258-9
Rowland Bingham: Into Africa's Interior • 978-1-57658-282-4
Ida Scudder: Healing Bodies, Touching Hearts • 978-1-57658-285-5
Wilfred Grenfell: Fisher of Men • 978-1-57658-292-3
Lillian Trasher: The Greatest Wonder in Egypt • 978-1-57658-305-0
Loren Cunningham: Into All the World • 978-1-57658-199-5
Florence Young: Mission Accomplished • 978-1-57658-313-5
Sundar Singh: Footprints Over the Mountains • 978-1-57658-318-0
C.T. Studd: No Retreat • 978-1-57658-288-6
Rachel Saint: A Star in the Jungle • 978-1-57658-337-1
Brother Andrew: God's Secret Agent • 978-1-57658-355-5
Clarence Jones: Mr. Radio • 978-1-57658-343-2
Count Zinzendorf: Firstfruit • 978-1-57658-262-6
John Wesley: The World His Parish • 978-1-57658-382-1
C. S. Lewis: Master Storyteller • 978-1-57658-385-2
David Bussau: Facing the World Head-on • 978-1-57658-415-6
Jacob DeShazer: Forgive Your Enemies • 978-1-57658-475-0
Isobel Kuhn: On the Roof of the World • 978-1-57658-497-2
Elisabeth Elliot: Joyful Surrender • 978-1-57658-513-9
D. L. Moody: Bringing Souls to Christ • 978-1-57658-552-8
Paul Brand: Helping Hands • 978-1-57658-536-8
Dietrich Bonhoeffer: In the Midst of Wickedness • 978-1-57658-713-3
Francis Asbury: Circuit Rider • 978-1-57658-737-9

Samuel Zwemer: The Burden of Arabia • *978-1-57658-738-6*
Klaus-Dieter John: Hope in the Land of the Incas • *978-1-57658-826-2*
Mildred Cable: Through the Jade Gate • *978-1-57658-886-4*
John Flynn: Into the Never Never • *978-1-57658-898-7*
Richard Wurmbrand: Love Your Enemies • *978-1-57658-987-8*
Charles Mulli: We Are Family • *978-1-57658-894-9*
John Newton: Change of Heart • *978-1-57658-909-0*
Helen Roseveare: Mama Luka • *978-1-57658-910-6*
Norman Grubb: Mission Builder • *978-1-57658-915-1*
Albert Schweitzer • *978-1-57658-961-8*

Heroes of History

George Washington Carver: From Slave to Scientist • *978-1-883002-78-7*
Abraham Lincoln: A New Birth of Freedom • *978-1-883002-79-4*
Meriwether Lewis: Off the Edge of the Map • *978-1-883002-80-0*
George Washington: True Patriot • *978-1-883002-81-7*
William Penn: Liberty and Justice for All • *978-1-883002-82-4*
Harriet Tubman: Freedombound • *978-1-883002-90-9*
John Adams: Independence Forever • *978-1-883002-50-3*
Clara Barton: Courage under Fire • *978-1-883002-51-0*
Daniel Boone: Frontiersman • *978-1-932096-09-5*
Theodore Roosevelt: An American Original • *978-1-932096-10-1*
Douglas MacArthur: What Greater Honor • *978-1-932096-15-6*
Benjamin Franklin: Live Wire • *978-1-932096-14-9*
Christopher Columbus: Across the Ocean Sea • *978-1-932096-23-1*
Laura Ingalls Wilder: A Storybook Life • *978-1-932096-32-3*
Orville Wright: The Flyer • *978-1-932096-34-7*
Captain John Smith: A Foothold in the New World • *978-1-932096-36-1*
Thomas Edison: Inspiration and Hard Work • *978-1-932096-37-8*
Alan Shepard: Higher and Faster • *978-1-932096-41-5*
Ronald Reagan: Destiny at His Side • *978-1-932096-65-1*
Davy Crockett: Ever Westward • *978-1-932096-67-5*
Milton Hershey: More Than Chocolate • *978-1-932096-82-8*
Billy Graham: America's Pastor • *978-1-62486-024-9*
Ben Carson: A Chance at Life • *978-1-62486-034-8*
Louis Zamperini: Redemption • *978-1-62486-049-2*
Elizabeth Fry: Angel of Newgate • *978-1-62486-064-5*
William Wilberforce: Take Up the Fight • *978-1-62486-057-7*
William Bradford: Plymouth's Rock • *978-1-62486-092-8*
Ernest Shackleton: Going South • *978-1-62486-093-5*
Benjamin Rush: The Common Good • *978-1-62486-123-9*
Dwight Eisenhower: Supreme Commander • *978-1-62486-142-0*

Available in paperback, e-book, and audiobook formats.
Unit Study Curriculum Guides are available for many biographies.
www.YWAMpublishing.com